ALSO BY GENE STONE

The Bush Survival Bible
Duck! The Dick Cheney Survival Bible

The 12-Step Bush Recovery Program

The
12-Step
Bush
Recovery
Program

*A Lifesaving Guide to Shaking Off the Horrors of
the Last Eight Years, with Practical Advice on
Relapse, Remission, and Recounts*

Gene Stone
with Carl Pritzkat and Tony Travostino

VILLARD NEW YORK

The 12-Step Bush Recovery Program is a work of nonfiction. None of the advice offered, however, can take the place of professional counsel, no matter how much you wish it could. Moreover, the Internet sites mentioned are subject to change, and the author and publisher make no representation as to the accuracy or dependability of any site referred to in this book, or any information on any such sites, or anything else. And please keep in mind that the jokes about George W. Bush do not represent reality. However, we do not claim to know what reality is.

*This book is dedicated to all those who now wish
they had voted for Al Gore and John Kerry*

CONTENTS

The 12-Step Bush Recovery Program

Step 1. Acknowledge the Problem

Hi. My name is Gene. Like you, I am now doing my best to recover from eight years of George Walker Bush, the forty-third president of the United States.

Some of you know exactly what I am talking about. But many of you are asking, What does he mean? What is he saying? Recovery? I don't drink a lot. I don't smoke a lot. I don't even shop a lot. I don't need recovery.

Yes, you do. You, too, need recovery from the eight years of the presidency of George W. Bush.

Where were you during these last eight years? Do you even remember? Probably not. It's all a haze of horribly hideous headlines, excruciating election evenings, and idiotic international incidents.

So, together, let's try to remember what happened: During these past eight years, this country has seen its citizens' civil liberties imperiled, its environment endangered, and its freedoms jeopardized. Nature reserves have been destroyed. Energy policy has favored enormous oil conglomerates over consumers. The financial markets have suffered some of their worst months since the Depression. Education for our children has been underfinanced while being tangled in red tape and test scores. The Supreme Court has been stacked with justices who were less than truthful in their confirmation hearings and have gone on to redefine judicial precedents. The Constitution, the basic framework of our government, has been mocked and abused.

It's been a bad eight years for culture, music, and television, too.

Now are you beginning to remember? Are you overcoming your forgetfulness? Is it all becoming clear? Are you becoming conscious of your Bush-induced insanity?

And what were you doing throughout all those years? Were you fighting to stop these things from happening, doing everything you could to limit the damage? Or were you repressing your ill feelings and sitting on your hands?

To get a better sense of your true emotional state, take this simple test. Grab a pen and circle the words in the list below that best represent your feelings about the Bush years:

Anger   Fury   Resentment   Annoyance
Wrath   Bile   Rage   Dissatisfaction   Vexation
Discontent   Bitterness   Indignation
Degradation   Humiliation   Powerlessness
Regret   Wistfulness   Loathing   Repugnance
Abhorrence   Revulsion   Sullenness   Animosity
Hostility   Displeasure   Exasperation
Mortification   Shame

Now look closely at the words you have circled. Do you see a pattern? If more than a few of the words you chose

IT'S NOT MY FAULT THAT GEORGE W. BUSH WAS ELECTED. I NEVER VOTED FOR HIM. NOBODY CAN BLAME ME FOR THIS FIASCO. I AM TOTALLY INNOCENT. I AM OKAY.

It's very common, before you can admit your problem, to blame other people for it. The fact is, you could have done more to stop George Bush from being elected. You could have done more to stop Bush from being reelected. You will find, once you go into recovery, that blaming other people for your problem is never the answer. Blaming Republicans is.

indicate negative feelings, there is a strong likelihood that you are sitting on a large reservoir of anger and resentment. Don't let it destroy you. Admit the problem and move on to the solution!

Are you starting to believe me? What about one more test? Answer this short list of yes-or-no questions and see how you fare:

	YES	NO
Do you ever tell people overseas that things aren't nearly as bad as they think?	☐	☐
Do you wake up in the morning and pretend it's 1999?	☐	☐
Did you stop donating money to left-wing causes?	☐	☐
Did you ever "forget" to protest the war?	☐	☐
Do you indulge in fantasies that the Supreme Court is fair and just?	☐	☐
Do you ever use liquor to ease the pain induced by American politics?	☐	☐
Do you watch DVDs of *The West Wing* and pretend Martin Sheen is the real president?	☐	☐
Do you ever watch Fox News and believe it really is news?	☐	☐
Do you think the damage done to this country in the past eight years is minimal?	☐	☐
Do you wish Jeb Bush could become president?	☐	☐
Do you wish Jenna Bush could become president?	☐	☐
Do you wish Barbara Bush could become president?	☐	☐

If you answered yes to one or more of these questions, you probably need to enter a recovery program.

Are you ready to admit it now? Can you see through the miasma of forgetfulness? Do you want to know more about how bad it was?

Sean Wilentz, a professor of history at Princeton University, wrote in a 2006 article for *Rolling Stone* magazine that great presidents "rallied the nation, governed brilliantly and left the republic more secure than when they entered office. . . . Calamitous presidents, faced with enormous difficulties—James Buchanan, Andrew Johnson, [Herbert] Hoover, and now Bush—have divided the nation, governed erratically and left the nation worse off."

An informal survey of more than one hundred professional historians, conducted under the auspices of the History News Network, revealed that 98.2 percent of them regarded George W. Bush's presidency as a failure. Moreover, 61 percent of them ranked Bush as the "worst ever" president.

For those of you who still do not comprehend this concept, realize that you are living in denial. You don't recognize that you have a problem.

Here's a well-known fact common to all recovery programs: Denying the problem is the first sign of having one.

Here's another well-known fact: Denial never works. Denial always ends up creating more and more denial, until you spiral into oblivion.

So it's time to leave all this denial behind and admit the truth: You, and this country, have been in a terrible haze for the last eight years, and it's time to take the appropriate steps to recover.

There is no such thing as a problem without a solu-

PAST EXCUSES

Part of the process of recovery is the act of taking responsibility both for your past behavior and for your future direction. That means no more hiding behind excuses.

Here is a list of excuses and arguments that, as a recoverer, you will no longer be able to use:

- I can't make it to that meeting, Boss, that's when I have my one-hundred-mile midday bike ride.
- You're going to have to reschedule that business trip because I'm on vacation from June to August . . . every year.
- If the president doesn't know how to read, I'm sure as hell not going to learn.
- Sorry to have to waterboard you, Steve, but this isn't cruel and unusual punishment, and you still haven't told me where you put my scissors.
- Why should I try to get A's? The president was a C student.
- I'm the decider. End of conversation.

tion—at least, not in the world of recovery. There is always hope.

Not that recovery from the Bush years will be easy. Just as any journey has its ups and its downs, its rewards and its hazards, its progressives and its conservatives, so will this journey.

However, there is good news. You are not alone. There are many other people just like you. In fact, there are approximately three hundred million of you, all facing the same difficult issue.

Even better news, if you have picked up this book you are open to the idea that you have a problem. You are starting to admit that these last eight years have caused enormous damage. You are beginning to understand that you let your power slip away from you and that, in the process, life became unmanageable.

Instead of running from the problem, you are now seeking a healthy solution. You are seeking recovery. You needn't be ashamed. You needn't hide this book from the checkout clerk. A new life—a happier life—awaits you.

This program was loosely adapted from 12-step programs designed to treat other types of issues. Besides the twelve steps themselves, you will find twelve guest speakers, who have come to the Bush Recovery Program to discuss momentous topics such as recovery for the environment and humor.

You now understand that only with outside help can you recover from your Bush-induced insanity. You are ready to move on to Step 2.

— *Guest Speaker Jonathan Z. Larsen on* —

THE ENVIRONMENT

Jonathan Z. Larsen is a journalist and environmentalist. He has been an editor and Saigon bureau chief at Time, *news editor at* Life, *and editor in chief of* New Times *and* The Village Voice, *and served on the editorial boards of the* Columbia Journalism Review, Nuclear Times, *and* OnEarth. *He is also an honorary trustee of the Natural Resources Defense Council and is currently building a no-carbon solar and geothermal house in Vermont.*

It is not too much of stretch to claim that George W. Bush won the presidency with a lie about the environment. Throughout his 2000 campaign, he pledged to cap carbon emissions, a remarkable concession from a second-generation Texas oilman. This lie effectively co-opted Al Gore's biggest issue.

Once elected, Bush welshed on that promise and set about to hobble the Department of the Interior, the Environmental Protection Agency, and other environmental watchdog agencies by stuffing them with oil and auto lobbyists, party hacks, and religious quacks. Author Carl Hiaasen called Bush appointee Gale Norton "the worst Interior Secretary in modern history."

Meanwhile, Dick Cheney was famously meeting behind closed doors with the world's biggest polluters to determine how the Bush administration could make them happy. The result was lax enforcement and general incompetence across the board.

Bush's two terms have been marked by rampant corruption in oil and gas leases, by public land giveaways, and by the manipulation and suppression of information. Worse, as president, Bush utterly failed to use his bully pulpit to address two of the biggest threats facing the country: global warming—the effects of those carbon emissions he refused to cap—and the country's staggering dependence on foreign oil, which in turn has created the largest transfer of wealth in history from the United States to our current and future enemies.

Thanks to a dedicated opposition in Congress and the unflagging efforts of the nongovernmental organizations (NGOs) in the field, his attempt to roll back thirty-five years of environmental regulation has largely failed. The next president, the Congress, and the federal agencies will have to do much better going forward to make up for the lost eight years.

Indeed, citizens also have to do a lot better. Here is what you can do, both to recover from the Bush calamity and to help your nation move forward.

1. Buy a pair of solar hot water panels, put them on your roof, and take a long, restorative shower.
2. Hurt Dick Cheney's feelings by intensifying your personal ethic of conservation and recycling.
3. Put your money where your heart is: Support your favorite environmental organizations and invest in top-performing socially responsible funds. Last year, these included Ariel (ARGFX) and Pax World (Balanced—PAXWV).
4. Using recycled paper, write letters to the White House and your local representatives at home and in Washington in support of environmental legislation.

5. Go out of your way to hug a scientist, an economist, an environmentalist—these have been the most endangered species over the last eight years.
6. Give the grid a break. As often as possible, turn off the trickle-power transformer on your cell phone charger and the standby power on your cable/satellite receiver, your audio system, and your microwave.
7. In 1931, Thomas Edison declared, "I'd put my money on the sun and solar energy. What a source of power." It is not too late to follow his advice.
8. Pray that the League of Conservation Voters will give the next president an A on the environment. They gave George W. Bush an F, the lowest score the organization has ever given.

Step 2. Understand What You've Been Through

Now that you're willing to admit you have an issue that demands attention, you can concentrate on trying to grasp the scope of that issue.

During your eight-year George W. Bush–induced insanity, you might even have gotten to the point where you forgot what things were like before that haze descended. This symptom is typical of people who have not been completely conscious of their recent actions.

For example, can you remember that before the problem with George W. Bush began, this nation wasn't in a constant state of war and fear? In fact, during the eight years prior to this Bush administration, fewer than one hundred Americans were killed overseas. But in the eight years of George W. Bush's presidency, more than four thousand were killed in Iraq alone.

Can you recall that before George W. Bush, the federal government had a budget surplus of $559 billion? Now it's got a deficit of $482 billion. In fact, during his eight years in office, Bush has increased the national debt

MY WIFE WON'T LEAVE ME ALONE. SHE KEEPS
TELLING ME THAT MY BEHAVIOR HAS BECOME
IRRATIONAL AND THAT LIVING WITH ME HAS
BECOME DIFFICULT. I FIND THIS ABSURD. I ONLY
SMASH THE TELEVISION SET A FEW TIMES A WEEK
NOW. SO AREN'T I FINE?

No.

by $4 trillion—due in part to his tax cuts, which favored the wealthiest 1 percent of the population. People making more than $1 million annually received, on average, $150,000 a year in Bush tax breaks, as opposed to the average American, who received about $750 a year from the cuts.

The median American household income grew by more than 2 percent in the eight years prior to George W. Bush. After eight years of George W. Bush, it has declined by more than 1 percent. A gallon of gas was once $1.50; now it costs in the neighborhood of $4.00. A gallon of milk used to cost $2.75; it's also around $4.00 now.

This tally might be a painful exercise, but it's important that you dig into your memory to recall further transgressions.

Do you remember when torture wasn't something for which Americans were famous? When the Geneva conventions and the United Nations were concepts that we supported—and that we *initiated*—rather than bothersome technicalities that we dodged?

There was a time when we all knew that no matter what happened we had the right to remain silent, the right to have a lawyer present, and the right to a fair and speedy trial, instead of wondering whether an unauthorized government tap on our phone might lead to our being detained in an undisclosed location where we would be subjected to "enhanced interrogation techniques."

Keep looking back in time—it may be upsetting, but covering up those years will only bring more pain. It's difficult, but you can get through this.

Recall that before George W. Bush came into your life, health insurance was generally paid for by your employer. It was a time when you didn't have to decide whether you would continue to pay your health insurance premiums, which are up 140 percent since Bush came into office, or risk living without insurance and being bankrupted by illness.

Can you remember that before Bush, Medicare was regarded as a program designed to help retired Americans with their health-care expenses, as opposed to Bush's Medicare prescription drug program, which actually increased prescription drug costs for many Medicare recipients?

Now dig even deeper into your memory—to a time when government agencies enforced laws instead of trying to dismantle them. Go back to when the courts stood by their legal reasoning, rather than saying, as the Supreme Court did in 2000, in the case of *Bush v. Gore,* that their decision should set no precedent. Go back to when the government still defended individual rights, as opposed to arguing, like the Bush administration did, that certain people should have to prove they are allowed to vote (*Crawford v. Marion County Election Board*); or that women don't have the right to control what happens to their own bodies (*Gonzales v. Carhart* and *Gonzales v. Planned Parenthood*); or that the accused, rather than being innocent until proven guilty, have no right to a fair hearing (*Rumsfeld v. Padilla*).

It may be harder to recall when scientists, and the scientific method, were driving government efforts to clean up the environment, halt the advance of climate change, and prevent the spread of HIV/AIDS—as opposed to the political hacks, right-wing fundamentalists, and big-industry stooles who have derailed those efforts. Or to remember when stem cell research was encouraged for its potential to conquer life-threatening illnesses such as can-

STAGING AN INTERVENTION

What can you do when someone you love refuses to enter Bush recovery?

You stage what is known as an intervention.

An intervention is a meeting in which family, friends, and, sometimes, a professional therapist or counselor assemble to help an individual who has a problem. The subject is made aware, often for the first time, of how deeply he or she needs help. Consequently, interventions enjoy a high rate of success.

People often don't realize just how much they have been suffering vis-à-vis Bush. So if you have a loved one who isn't aware of the problem, help the person. Ask a friend, a member of the clergy, or just a clear thinker to join you. Sit down with your loved one and ask these questions: Are you aware of how horrible the Bush years have been? Are you willing to do something about the sorry state of this country?

Don't be surprised if these questions provoke tears in your loved one. People who have been sleeping through these last eight years are often jolted when they are forced to face reality. "Oh my God," goes a typical response. "You mean he's been president for all these years and I never noticed?"

Now, sometimes people don't agree to get help. They'll say, "You may be right, but I can handle the problem on my own." You must not accept this. You need to get your loved one help. If you must, use your weapon of last resort. Ask: Do you want to endure another four years of this kind of government? That usually does the trick.

cer, leukemia, and Parkinson's disease, and faith-based concepts such as intelligent design weren't proposed as a viable alternative to real science.

It's important to understand just how far down George W. Bush has taken you, because it will help you make sure that you never fall that far again. That you never return to the time when funding was cut for our schools, their curricula becoming fixated on passing Bush-mandated tests, and the nation's international ranking for math scores plummeting to thirty-fifth, between Russia and Croatia. That you never again have to witness the destruction of one of the nation's largest and most beloved cities because the federal agency tasked with its rescue was incapable of responding. That you never again have to suffer the embarrassment of watching the world's greatest military force, mismanaged by incompetence, being sent off to a fabricated war without adequate or appropriate support.

Yes, it's important to understand what you've just been through, and even more important that you never forget it. Otherwise, you might not be able to fully recover. Worse yet, you may well have to experience it all over again.

You've just completed a difficult, agonizing step. Take several long, deep breaths before moving on to Step 3.

MONEY

Andrew Tobias is the author of, among a dozen other books, the perennial bestseller The Only Investment Guide You'll Ever Need. *He has also been a columnist for* Time, New York, *and* Parade *magazines as well as a pioneer in personal finance computer software, cohost of the PBS series* Beyond Wall Street, *a crusader against the tobacco industry, a recipient of the Consumer Federation of America Media Service Award, and grand marshal of New York's Gay Pride Parade. A graduate of Harvard College and Harvard Business School, for the past decade he has served as Treasurer of the Democratic National Committee.*

Nothing went wrong with the economy from Bush and Cheney's point of view—it was a grand time to be rich in America. Better still to be an oil man. In eight years, the stock price of oil field servicer Halliburton quintupled. Taxes for the ultra rich were slashed (billionaires are now in a lower tax bracket than their manicurists) even as middle class incomes fell and the cost of life's necessities soared.

At the kitchen table, where the bills are paid, times are grim. At the macro level, Bush put us in a terrible box. Promising a balanced budget, he borrowed four trillion dollars from your grandchildren. Our national debt, accumulated since 1776, will have reached ten trillion dollars by the time he leaves office. Of that, eight trillion will have been racked up under just three of our 43 presidents: Reagan, Bush, and Bush. A manageable 30 percent of GDP when Reagan took office, the debt will be 75 percent when Bush leaves—and is headed straight up.

Even now, just the *interest* we pay on that mostly Republican National Debt exceeds 40 percent of all the personal income taxes we pay. Imagine what would happen if the markets started demanding higher rates to hold our bonds. In short: Bush ended "the American Century" right on time.

Things you can do to recover:

1. **Live light on the land.** Almost all the things that save *you* money and enhance your own financial security (and often, your health) also reduce the drain on our collective wealth.
   - Walk or bike short distances instead of drive.
   - Eat local produce; eat chicken instead of beef; eat *less.*
   - Turn the lights off when you leave the room.
   - Turn the television off when no one's watching.
   - Turn the heat way down or the air conditioner way up when no one's home.
   - Wrap gifts with newspaper instead of wrapping paper.
   - Quit smoking.
   - Use less detergent—you'd be surprised how little does the trick.
   - Let clothes dry in the sun.
   - Buy a nondisposable water bottle, once, and keep refilling it from the tap. Americans discard thirty billion plastic water bottles (made from petroleum) each year.

      The list is endless. Go to the library (don't buy it) and get my book.

2. **Live beneath your means.** That way, you come out ahead each year, accumulating wealth for the future (and, through your investments, helping to finance our economic resurgence). Pay off your credit cards! Buy generics! Cut your own hair! Set goals and make a budget to reach them so it all becomes part of your grand recovery plan. (Did I mention going to the library to read more about all this?)

3. **Keep your transaction costs low.** That's the one piece of the investment puzzle you can control. Mutual funds with very low expenses (e.g., at Vanguard, whose index funds have an all-in cost of about 20 basis points, or 20 hundredths of 1 percent) are like horses with twenty-pound jockeys. They may not always win; but against typical mutual funds, with 200-pound jockeys (counting all expenses and fees), they give you a huge advantage. Likewise: simple-to-shop-for low-expense term life insurance instead of impossible to price-compare fancier life insurance products (and expense-laden annuities). Likewise: deep-discount brokers, like Ameritrade or Fidelity, if you buy individual stocks, instead of ten-times-more-expensive "full-service" brokers.

4. **Diversify** (if you're lucky enough to have appreciable assets, as few do) both in asset class (cash, stocks, real estate, etc.) and geographically. Who says the United States dollar will always outperform all other currencies—under Bush, it lost close to half its value. If you have a lot of cash, why hold it all in American dollars? If you have mutual funds, why restrict yourself to those that invest only in American securities?

5. **Take full advantage of any employer-matched 401(k)** and/or, next on the retirement pecking order,

set up and fully fund a Roth IRA at a consumer friendly financial supermarket like Vanguard or T Rowe Price.

6. **Vote Democrat.** Seriously. The economy and the stock market do significantly better under Democratic administrations. You can look it up.

Step 3. Deal with Embarrassment

Now that you're beginning to remember what you've been through during these past eight years, you need to reflect on some of your individual actions that contributed to the trouble—embarrassing, humiliating, foolish, and otherwise.

Until you actually enter a Bush Recovery Group, you won't be able to say these things aloud. You are, however, highly encouraged to make a list of any and all of your transgressions from these years and read the list to yourself. Then weep.

The good news is that no matter what you have done, no matter how low you have sunk, there is someone who has done something worse and sunk even lower than you. Get a grip on your ego and stop punishing yourself—yes, you might have said and done some things that you regret but now try to gain some perspective by learning about the transgressions of others.

Nothing gives us better perspective than an awareness of the frailty of the human condition—or its stupidity, for that matter.

For instance, in late 2006 a Texas farmer named Craig Baker became so enraged that a mosque was being built next to his property that he started staging pig races on his land every Friday, one of Islam's holiest days, to get revenge. Up to one hundred people attended the races, but the ploy did not deter construction of the mosque. As the president of the local Islamic Association pointed out, pig races were not offensive to the members of his association. Muslims do not hate pigs. They just don't eat them.

Meanwhile, in Ohio, twenty-nine-year-old Eric Richley was apparently so overwhelmed by the attacks of September 11, 2001, that, somewhat inebriated, he rammed his car into the Grand Mosque at the Islamic Center of Greater Cleveland at eighty miles per hour. The car smashed into the mosque's steps and flew six feet into the air before crashing into the building. Richley later told the police that he had only intended to commit suicide. A disbelieving judge sentenced him to five years in jail for burglary, ethnic intimidation, and driving under the influence. No one was hurt at the mosque except Richley, who is now in a wheelchair. He also lost his driver's license.

During the francophobic fervor of the early 2000s, which resulted in French fries being renamed "freedom fries" in congressional cafeterias, many others took out their animosity on wine. For example, Ken Wagner, a bar owner in West Palm Beach, Florida, emptied his entire stock of French wine and champagne into the gutter, saying that from now on he would serve "vintages only from nations that support U.S. policy." This meant that Mr. Wagner was now free to serve vintage wines from such willing countries as Poland, Bulgaria, Mongolia, and Tonga.

MAYBE THESE LAST FEW YEARS HAVE BEEN TOUGH, BUT THEY COULD HAVE BEEN WORSE. AFTER ALL, MY LAWN IS STILL GREEN, I CAN DRINK MY TAP WATER, AND THE ENORMOUS OIL DERRICK SPEWING VILE CRAP OUTSIDE MY OCEAN-VIEW WINDOW HAS BECOME VERY ATTRACTIVE TO ME. DO I REALLY HAVE A PROBLEM?

Each person's definition of a problem is different. Some people grasp their problem quickly, others don't. Also, what is a problem to some is not a problem to others. Maintaining objectivity is difficult in this area. Skilled practitioners must always be careful not to judge. However, you have a problem.

Then there's the case of former U.S. Representative Curt Weldon, a Republican from Pennsylvania and an ardent believer that Iraq possessed weapons of mass destruction (WMD)—even after the Bush administration itself stopped pretending they existed. When Dave Gaubatz, a former Air Force special investigator, approached Weldon with what he called new evidence about WMD, the congressman insisted on going to Iraq to uncover the weapons himself, under the guise of visiting troops. Once there, Gaubatz said, Weldon planned to persuade the U.S. military commander to lend him the equipment and men to go digging along the Euphrates River. Unfortunately for Mr. Weldon, he lost his next election and therefore his chance to dig in the sand.

Thinking even bigger than Mr. Weldon is Domino's Pizza founder Tom Monaghan, who, taking to heart the Bush administration's call for more religion in our daily lives, is establishing what amounts to a Catholic utopia. Called Ave Maria and located near Naples, Florida, the community includes a university, a law school, seventeen tennis courts, a golf course, and an activities director. Monaghan had originally stated that commercial leases in the town would enforce Catholic beliefs, including prohibiting the sale of pornography and contraceptives and banning abortions. When the American Civil Liberties Union (ACLU) announced it would oppose these plans in court, Monaghan backed off from some of them—for now.

And speaking of religion, when George W. Bush said that the jury was still out on evolution, he prompted school boards around the country to add creationism to their science curricula, including one in Dover, Pennsylvania. In October 2004 the Dover school board voted six to three to include the following statement about creationism in the district's ninth grade biology classes: "Because Darwin's theory is a theory, it continues to be tested as new evidence is discovered. The theory is not a fact. Gaps in the theory exist for which there is no evidence. . . . Intelligent design is an explanation of the origin of life that differs from Darwin's view."

The decision didn't sit well with many people: Numerous teachers refused to read the statement in their classrooms, and the law was quickly challenged in court. But before a judge's decision was rendered, the citizens of the Dover Area School District awoke from their Bush-induced haze and voted all six school board members who had supported the statement out of office.

Other people took different embarrassing actions. In the wake of anthrax attacks in Washington and New York and warnings from the Department of Homeland Security to secure homes with duct tape, one Connecticut man wrapped his entire house in plastic. Paul West, of Winsted, Connecticut, bought hundreds of feet of plastic sheeting, batten boards, staple guns, and ladders to use in sealing his home. "I just have all this energy from tension and anxiety and I don't know what to do with it," West told reporters in 2003. "Basically, I'm doing what the government says we should do."

Immediately after September 11, 2001, many airline passengers' nerves were frayed. However, a full six years later, Leigh Robbins, a housewife from Richmond, Virginia, was so scared to fly that she demanded the plane she had boarded be prevented from leaving the ground so she could get off because she refused to share the flight with seven male passengers who looked Arabic. (The men were Iraq-born American citizens who had been in California helping to train the American military.) The men were doing nothing to warrant suspicion, but the flight was consequently delayed for twelve hours while the Iraqis were questioned and then released. Ms. Robbins was late returning home.

So as you reflect on your own worst behavior patterns from the last eight years, consider that, yes, you enabled George W. Bush to invade Iraq, to appoint far-right-wing Supreme Court justices, to destroy the American dollar, and so on. But at least you didn't end up as fodder for late-night talk show monologues.

SLURRED SPEECH PATTERNS

The warning signs that indicate the need for a recovery program are varied. They range from limited ambulation to difficulty in breathing, from night sweats to hallucinations, from violence to sleeplessness.

Certainly one common indicator is limited speaking ability. Following are some examples of what poor verbalization patterns can sound like to other people. Coincidentally, all of these quotes were uttered by George W. Bush.

"Rarely is the question asked: Is our children learning?" (January 11, 2000)

"I know the human being and fish can coexist peacefully." (September 29, 2000)

"They misunderestimated me." (November 6, 2000)

"Families is where our nation finds hope, where wings take dream." (October 18, 2000)

"I just want you to know that, when we talk about war, we're really talking about peace." (June 18, 2002)

"There's an old saying in Tennessee—I know it's in Texas, probably in Tennessee—that says, fool me once, shame on—shame on you. Fool me—you can't get fooled again." (September 17, 2002)

"Our enemies are innovative and resourceful, and so are we. They never stop thinking about new ways to harm our country and our people, and neither do we." (August 5, 2004)

"The question is, who ought to make that decision? The Congress or the commanders? And as you know, my position is clear—I'm a commander guy." (May 2, 2007)

"I heard somebody say, 'Where's [Nelson] Mandela?' Well, Mandela's dead. Because Saddam killed all the Mandelas." (September 20, 2007)

"Goodbye from the world's biggest polluter." (July 10, 2008, his parting words to fellow G-8 leaders at a summit meeting)

"And they have no disregard for human life." (July 15, 2008, speaking about Afghan fighters)

WOMEN

Gail Evans, the former executive vice president of the CNN News Group, is currently a visiting professor at the Georgia Tech College of Management, where she teaches a course in gender, race, and ethnicity in organizational behavior, and a columnist at Pink *magazine. The bestselling author of* Play Like a Man, Win Like a Woman *(Broadway Books, 2000) and* She Wins, You Win *(Gotham Books, 2003), she is one of the country's foremost lecturers on women's issues.*

January 2009 means that once again "W" can stand for *women.* The end of the Bush administration will allow women to get to work to reverse the retreat on women's rights.

We have seen a White House press secretary declare that the president doesn't feel that discrimination against women is as serious as racial or ethnic discrimination. We have seen the global gag rule reinstated, cutting off funding to organizations that offer counseling on abortion. Foreign policy and the administration's antiabortion position have been joined, making it virtually impossible for relief agencies to give out birth control information if they receive any funding from the government. Every program that enhances gender equality has been eroded during the Bush years: Title IX, which has given women and girls a fairer chance in college athletics, has been weakened. The power of the Women's Bureau of the Department of Labor has been diminished. The Bush-packed Supreme Court has made it more difficult for victims of wage discrimination to file and win lawsuits. The lower courts have been packed with judges determined to advance his antichoice agenda.

To recover, here are the steps we need to take:

1. Women of different political stripes need to work together to make real progress for ourselves and our daughters.
2. We must rely on facts and science to move our agenda forward, not on emotion and ideology.
3. We must look toward the future and not get stuck in complaining about past injustices.
4. We must think globally again and remember that the emergence of women in every society is a victory for all of us.
5. Women must stop waiting for the perfect issue that is exactly what they want and, instead, understand that politics is about compromise, and that our voices must be heard on every issue, not just the traditional family ones.
6. We must elect more women. Currently the United States is sixty-first in the world in the number of female elected officials. Sixty-first! We need to be at the political table in larger numbers so that our voices are heard on issues from war to energy policy.

Step 4. Acknowledge a Higher Power

You've now made it through the first three steps. Well done! You have admitted that you have a problem, and you are coping with the truth about your past—as well as that of other people in your situation. You know that you are not alone, and you know that you need outside help to move on.

We now come to the next, very important, step. In fact, this might well be the most important one of all. This is the step at which we learn that our own personal concerns, from our problems to our recovery, are not as important as the larger issues of life.

Once upon a time in America, people had faith in something other than the person who held the office of president. There was a conviction that united our country and gave us hope when life's problems became thorny and when times were grim. After all, the eternal question for humankind isn't "Who are your leaders?" or "What shape is your country in?" That all-important question has always been: "What gives your life meaning?"

The answer is: Belief in something or someone greater

than yourself. Belief in a power that has lasted longer than any one person, and a power that will outlast anyone who holds the presidency, or any other post, today. A power larger and more profound than George W. Bush—in fact, a power that can right the wrongs that Bush has caused us to wreak upon ourselves.

What is that power?

The United States Constitution.

Before any of our current problems existed—before Hurricane Katrina, before the Iraq war, before the mortgage crisis, before $4-a-gallon gasoline, and before Harriet Miers—there was the U.S. Constitution.

When President Richard Nixon tried to claim executive privilege to avoid turning over incriminating tapes during the Watergate scandal, the Constitution was there to give the Supreme Court the power to say, unanimously, that no one person, not even the president, is above the law.

As far back as 1800, just eleven years after its creation, the Constitution was there for Thomas Jefferson, who used its power as his rallying cry to end the newly passed Alien and Sedition Acts, which suppressed criticism of the government.

In what might have been the Constitution's greatest test—and its greatest triumph—President Abraham Lincoln used its power to hold together a nation and end the national disgrace of slavery.

In fact, the Constitution was created by our forefathers to handle crises exactly like those George W. Bush has wrought. Many of these crises would never have taken place had we not strayed from the principles of our higher power.

Do you remember the first time you saw photographs of Abu Ghraib and the embarrassment you felt? But instead of letting your higher power, with its Eighth

Amendment ban on "cruel and unusual punishments" guide you, did you listen to George W. Bush's excuses?

What happened when it came time to determine crucial national priorities? You had a sinking feeling when you weren't allowed to know which industry insiders were setting our energy policy or why environmental laws were being ignored. But you let George W. Bush sway you, even though your higher power, the Constitution, clearly states that the president must "take care that the laws [enacted by Congress] be faithfully executed," to say nothing of the oath of office, whereby the president swore to "protect and defend the Constitution."

Take the nation to war? The Constitution says that Congress, not the president, has the power to declare war and that the president's foreign policy powers are granted "by and with the Advice and Consent of the Senate." But George W. Bush's influence over you allowed him to cajole the Congress, using fear and false information to launch a war.

The Constitution honors the importance of voting rights: "The right of citizens of the United States to vote shall not be denied or abridged." Yet you allowed Bush to erode them through bogus identification requirements in Indiana, deceitful purges of voting rolls in Florida, and misinformation campaigns aimed at sending the unwanted to the wrong polling places on the wrong dates in Ohio.

The Constitution honors and protects the place of religion in society by keeping it separate from government. George W. Bush violated this separation by favoring certain religious practices with government grants and endorsements, giving preferred denominations influence over the lives of other citizens.

The Constitution honors and encourages the free

exchange of discourse and debate by protecting against any attempts at "abridging the freedom of speech, or of the press" or curtailing our ability to "petition the Government for a redress of grievances." However, George W. Bush's influence over you has enabled channels of differing opinion to be constricted and voices that speak out against Bush policies to be vilified.

And the most fundamental power that the Constitution provides—"the right of the people to be secure in their persons, houses, papers, and effects, against unreasonable searches and seizures"—oh, how George W. Bush made you squander that right, through unsanctioned suspension of habeas corpus, illegal wiretaps, and kidnapping and torture of suspects.

Is this rock bottom? Could you sink any lower?

There is no need! The Constitution provides, if you give yourself over to its powers.

The Constitution is a contract between every American and our government. It is the oldest, and most successful, contract of its kind in the world. Its legal power supersedes that of any religious document, but that same legal power also guarantees personal freedom, such that any religious doctrine can have supreme power over any individual's life if the person so chooses. It provides the framework for our society, and it gives us all of the tools we need to govern.

Does it allow any room for interpretation? Yes—all documents, by nature, must do so. But its basic tenets resonate through American history, through every American's spirit, and through the dreams of people throughout the world.

Once you truly give yourself over to the powers of the Constitution, you'll never again feel the urge to subject yourself to the dark spell of George W. Bush.

INSANITY LIST

Sometimes, before going into full recovery mode, we do terrible things that we later regret, although at the time these actions seemed sensible. Make a list of some of the foolish things you did during the Bush years.

Here is a sample list:

I bought my children SUVs when they learned to drive.

I started building a nuclear reactor.

I sent Bush a birthday card.

I believed that torture produced reliable intelligence.

I was convinced that my son's/daughter's/brother's/sister's/friend's gay partnership threatened my own marriage.

I avoided paying my property tax by claiming that I'd moved to another state, even though I didn't really reside there.

I complained about paying the local school tax because my children were in private school.

I believed that Iraq was the source of the attacks of September 11.

I called someone a liberal in a not-nice way.

I believed Rush Limbaugh was taking drugs for real physical pain.

I thought Ann Coulter was smart.

I thought Ann Coulter was pretty.

I flew the flag even in the rain, thinking that patriotism overruled the Flag Code.

I went shopping to help the economy.

Matthew Yglesias, who started blogging when he was a teenager, is one of the most important and respected bloggers of his generation. He is currently a senior editor at the Center for American Progress, and his first book, Heads in the Sand, *was published by Wiley in 2008. Previously, he was an associate editor at* The Atlantic Monthly *and a staff writer at* The American Prospect. *In 2006, he was named* Playboy *magazine's blogger of the year.*

The Bush years have been a time of double crisis for the American media. Financially, the news business has never been in worse shape—with newspapers facing declining circulation, declining profits, tanking stock values, and staff cutbacks across the board. Substantively, too, the outlook has been bleak. The press spent most of the 2000 election—in retrospect, one of history's most consequential—assuring us that there were few important differences between the candidates and making fun of Al Gore for saying he'd invented the Internet, even though he never said any such thing.

Following the election's dubious resolution, we were assured that Bush would govern as a moderate (he didn't), then we were treated to post-9/11 hagiography, to a prewar period in which the press saw its job as to amplify the administration's dishonest case for an invasion of Iraq rather than to question the powerful, and to another presidential election campaign dominated by trivia and a political press lusting after the Democratic nominee's blood.

Nor does the stage appear to be set for any kind of improvement. As the current campaign unfolds, we've seen the Associated Press dub John McCain a "man of the people" for riding to Philadelphia in a first-class Acela train car, lacerate Hillary Clinton for not releasing her income tax returns while letting Cindy McCain get away with doing the same thing, and concoct endless excuses for McCain's repeated gaffes, flip-flops, lies, and misstatements.

But there is good news. The same technological changes that are wrecking business models in the traditional media are making it easier (and cheaper) than ever before for independent media to distribute their product to a wider audience. Consequently, not-for-profit publications and organizations such as *Mother Jones, The American Prospect, The Nation,* the Center for Independent Media, and ProPublica are beefing up their investments in serious reporting.

At the same time, reporting and commentary alike are blossoming as never before in the blogosphere, be it through large (by blog standards) outfits like Talking Points Memo, the Huffington Post, and Daily Kos or thousands of small grassroots operations.

What can you do to recover?

1. Read independent media.
2. Don't just read independent media; give some money to independent media. Without money, independent sources of information will vanish.
3. Don't believe everything you read, especially about the next supposedly dire threat to American security.
4. Demand better. Tell CNN and the Sunday morning chat shows that you're tired of watching panels where

progressive voices are drowned out two to one—if they're heard at all—and you're not going to watch anymore.

5. Write letters to the editor. They get read, and they make a difference.

6. If Rupert Murdoch owns it, don't watch it and don't subscribe to it.

Step 5. Undergo Detoxification

When treating any kind of addiction or dependence, the challenge of detoxification will arise. As you face reality, as you let go of the fantasies and images that have invaded your consciousness, your body and mind will change—you will rid yourself of the invaders, and you will begin to deal with the new you.

Detoxification can be frightening, challenging, and painful. When detoxing from an addiction such as alcohol, people often suffer delirium tremens—the notorious DTs—which can give you the shakes, nausea, and even hallucinations.

Detoxing from George W. Bush, however, requires something else: the ability to laugh. Have you realized how ridiculous this administration has been? If you haven't been laughing at it for the last eight years, it's time to catch up. The cathartic act of laughter helps to exterminate the toxic karma that has infected you. Laughter is, indeed, the best medicine for recovery, mostly because it doesn't need to be authorized by an HMO or an insurance company.

The following anecdotes must be read by all those who are making their way through the recovery process. In fact, it wouldn't hurt to read them over more than once, because you can't laugh at George W. Bush enough.

1. Before George W. Bush took over the presidency in 2001, Hillary and Bill Clinton invited him to the White House for a tour to help him acclimate.

    After drinking several glasses of iced tea, Bush asked President Clinton if he could use his personal bathroom. Clinton pointed him in the right direction, and Bush wandered off.

    When he entered the bathroom, he was astonished to see that President Clinton's urinal was made of gold.

    That afternoon, Bush told his wife, Laura, about the urinal and how much he looked forward to using it when he took over the presidency.

    Not long afterward, Laura and Hillary had tea together. Hillary asked what had impressed the Bushes most about their White House tour, so Laura mentioned how much her husband had admired the gold urinal.

    That evening, when Bill and Hillary were getting ready for bed, Hillary leaned over and whispered to Bill, "I found out who pissed in your saxophone."

2. Four doctors—from Tel Aviv, Berlin, Moscow, and Houston—were touring a new facility in China and started a conversation about the state of medicine in their own countries.

    The Israeli doctor said, "Medicine in my country is so advanced that we can take a kidney out of one man, put it in another, and have him looking for work in six weeks."

The German doctor said, "That is nothing. We can take a lung out of one person, put it in another, and have him looking for work in four weeks."

The Russian doctor said, "In my country, medicine is so advanced that we can take half a heart out of one person, put it in another, and have them both looking for work in two weeks."

The Texas doctor said, "I win. We recently took a man with no brain, put him in the White House for eight years, and now half the country is looking for work."

3. A guy walked into a bar and said to the bartender, "Isn't that George W. Bush and Colin Powell sitting over there in the corner?"

"Yes, that's them," the bartender said.

The guy decided to walk over and say hello. "This is a real honor," he said. "What are you guys doing in here?"

Having had several drinks, Bush's mouth was loose. "We're planning WWIII," he said.

The guy responded, "Really? What's going to happen?"

Bush replied "Well, we're going back to the Middle East, and this time we're going to kill forty million Iraqis, along with one bicycle repairman."

The guy looked confused. "A bicycle repairman! Why are you going to kill a bicycle repairman?"

Bush turned to Powell and smirked. "See, I told you no one was going to care about the forty million Iraqis!"

4. Back in Texas, George W. Bush bought himself a Corvette. One day he had trouble starting it, so he pushed it into a gas station and asked the mechanic for help.

The mechanic looked at it, did some tinkering, and in a few minutes it was working again.

"What's up?" Bush said.

"Just crap in the carburetor," the mechanic replied.

"How often do I have to do that?" Bush asked.

5. One day Albert Einstein, Pablo Picasso, and George W. Bush all showed up at the Pearly Gates for entry into heaven.

Einstein was first. St. Peter told him, "You certainly look like Einstein, but you have no idea what some people will do to sneak into Heaven. Can you prove that you really are Albert Einstein?"

Einstein quickly asked for a blackboard and some chalk. St. Peter gave it to him, and Einstein proceeded to draw a complicated description of relativity, general and special.

"Well," said St. Peter, "there's no question who you are. Welcome to heaven, Mr. Einstein."

Next, Picasso stepped forward, and again St. Peter asked how he could be sure that this man really was the famous artist. In reply, Picasso asked for the blackboard and chalk. St. Peter agreed, and Picasso immediately erased Einstein's equations and created a remarkable portrait of St. Peter.

St. Peter was suitably impressed. "Welcome to heaven, Mr. Picasso," he said.

Then George W. Bush cleared his throat. "Ahem," he said. "I'm George W. Bush."

I TAKE A LOT OF STIMULANTS, SMOKE A LOT OF WEED, AND ENJOY THE OCCASIONAL HALLUCINOGEN. IS IT POSSIBLE THAT I SIMPLY HALLUCINATED THE LAST EIGHT YEARS?

If that makes sense to you, it's quite possible you might be tripping right now. But if you really think it over, could your mind have come up with all the terrible things that happened? We think not.

St. Peter looked at him and said, "Both Einstein and Picasso were able to prove their identity. How can you prove yours?"

Bush's face went blank. "Who are Einstein and Picasso?" he asked.

St. Peter sighed. "Welcome to heaven, George," he said.

6. Dick Cheney, George W. Bush, and his father, George H. W. Bush, were all flying on Air Force One.

Dick looked at George W. and said, "You know, I could throw a hundred-dollar bill out the window right now and someone back on the ground would be very happy."

George W. shrugged his shoulders. "I could throw ten ten-dollar bills out the window and that would make ten people very happy."

George H. W. Bush then said, "Well, I could throw one hundred one-dollar bills out the window and make one hundred people happy."

Having heard enough, the pilot rolled her eyes, looked at all of them, and said, "I could throw all of you out the window and make the entire country happy."

7. George W. Bush and his two daughters decided they wanted some training as detectives, so they enrolled in a course.

To test her skill in recognizing a suspect, a detective showed Jenna a picture for five seconds and then hid it. "This is your suspect," he said. "Now, how would you recognize him if you saw him again?"

Jenna answered, "That's easy. He only has one eye!"

The policeman got a little angry. "That's because the picture only shows his profile," he said. "You need to pay more attention."

Jenna left the room and her sister entered. The detective flashed the picture at Barbara and asked the same question. "How would you recognize him?"

Barbara said, "Oh, he'd be very easy to find. He only has one ear."

The policeman responded, "What's the matter with you? Haven't you ever seen a profile before? Of course only one eye and one ear are showing!"

Barbara left, and then George W. came in for his test. The detective showed him the photo and asked, once again, "How would you recognize this man?"

Bush studied the picture very closely and then said, "The suspect wears contact lenses."

This answer surprised the policeman, who himself didn't know whether or not the suspect wore contacts.

"That's an interesting answer," he said. "Let me find his file." He left the room, went to his office, checked the suspect's file, and returned to the room, smiling.

"I have to admit, I'm amazed. The suspect does wear contact lenses. How in the world were you able to make such an astute observation?"

"Simple," Bush responded, "He can't wear regular glasses because he only has one eye and one ear."

8. After buying a brand new Rolls-Royce, a woman drove it home. Halfway there, she tried to change the radio station but failed. So she turned around and headed back to the dealer.

The dealer then explained that the radio was

a marvel of modern technology—it was a voice-activated station finder. All the woman had to do was say aloud the kind of music she wanted to hear, and the radio would find it for her.

Now the woman was even more excited by her car, so instead of driving home she rode around getting the music to change. First she said, "Classic rock," and soon she was hearing the Doobie Brothers. Then she said, "Baroque," and the music of Bach filled her car. She tried "Irish," and listened to Enya.

However, just as she tried another station, a fancy sports car ran a red light, and the woman had to slam on her brakes to avoid hitting it. She said angrily, "Asshole!"

And the radio cut to a George W. Bush press conference.

9. In light of all the criticism that George W. Bush is less than intelligent, the Republicans decided to hold a "George W. Bush Is Smart" convention, so they gathered fifty thousand Republicans in a football stadium.

Senator Trent Lott, the speaker, said, "We are all here today to prove to the world that George W. Bush is not stupid. So, ladies and gentlemen, let me introduce President George W. Bush."

After all the cheers died down, Senator Lott said, "Mr. President, we're going to prove to the world once and for all that you are not stupid. So tell us, what is fifteen plus fifteen?"

Bush, after scrunching up his face and concentrating, declared, "Eighteen!"

For a moment the crowd went silent. Then all fifty thousand started cheering, "Give Bush another chance! Give Bush another chance!"

So Senator Lott said, "America is the country of second chances. So here it is: What is five plus five?"

After nearly a minute of thinking, Bush said, "Twelve!"

Again, another moment of distressed silence, and then the crowd chanted, "Give Bush another chance! Give Bush another chance!"

Senator Lott decided to go along. "Okay, those were too tough. How about this one: What is two plus two?"

Bush looked down, counted on his fingers, hemmed and hawed, thought it over, and then said, "Four?"

Another moment of total silence. Then all fifty thousand Republicans jumped to their feet and screamed, "Give Bush another chance! Give Bush another chance!"

10. One day George W. Bush was out jogging and noticed a little boy on the corner with a box. Curious, he ran over to the child and said, "What's in the box, kid?"

The little boy said, "Kittens. My cat just had a whole litter of little kittens."

Bush laughed and said, "What kind of kittens are they?"

"Republicans," the child said.

"That's cute," Bush said, and he ran off.

A couple days later Bush was running with his buddy Dick Cheney and he spied the same boy on the corner with his box.

Bush told Dick, "You have to hear what this little boy has to say about his cats," and they both jogged over to the boy.

"Hey, kid," said Bush, "tell Dick what kind of kittens you have there."

The boy replied, "They're Democrats."

"Whoa!" George said. "When I came by here the other day, you said they were Republicans. What's up with that?"

"Well," the boy said, "Their eyes are open now."

11. George W. Bush was visiting an elementary school, talking about his presidency. Afterward, he invited the children to ask him a few questions.

Little Bobby got up and said, "Mr. President, I have got two questions to ask: First, how come you won the 2000 election, even though you had fewer votes than Gore? And second, why did you pretend there were weapons of mass destruction in Iraq?"

Just at that moment, the bell for the break rang and the children ran out of the classroom.

When the kids returned, Bush encouraged them once again to ask questions. This time little Susie rose to speak.

"Mr. President, I've got four questions to ask: First, how come you won the 2000 election, even though you had fewer votes than Gore? Second, why did you pretend there were weapons of mass destruction in Iraq? Third, why did the bell ring twenty minutes earlier today? And fourth, where is little Bobby?"

12. On a nice spring day in 2009, an old man walked up to the White House. Approaching the Marine stand-

ing guard, he said, "I'd like to go in and meet with President George W. Bush."

The Marine replied, "Sir, Mr. Bush is no longer president and doesn't reside here."

The old man said, "Okay," and walked away.

The following day, the same man approached the White House and said to the same Marine, "I would like to go in and meet with President George W. Bush."

The Marine again told the man, "Sir, as I said yesterday, Mr. Bush is no longer president and doesn't reside here."

The old man thanked him and walked away.

The next day the same man approached the same Marine and said the same thing: "I would like to go in and meet with President George W. Bush."

The Marine, becoming a little upset, said, "Sir, this is the third day in a row you have come here asking to speak to Mr. Bush. I've told you several times that Mr. Bush is not the president anymore and he doesn't reside here. Can't you understand?"

"I understand you perfectly well," the old man said. "I just love hearing your answer!"

The Marine snapped to attention and saluted. "See you tomorrow, sir!" he said.

Tony Hendra was recently described by The Independent *of London as "British comedy's great unsung talent . . . one of the most brilliant comic talents of the post-war period." He performed with John Cleese and Graham Chapman of* Monty Python's Flying Circus, *was an original editor of the* National Lampoon, *starred in the film* This Is Spinal Tap, *cocreated the long-running British satirical series* Spitting Image, *and has written or edited dozens of books and parodies, many of them huge bestsellers, including* Not The New York Times; The 80s: A Look Back at the Tumultuous Decade, 1980–1989; The Sayings of Ayatollah Khomeini; Off The Wall Street Journal; Going Too Far; Brotherhood, *a tribute to the firefighters of 9/11; and most recently* Father Joe: The Man Who Saved My Soul.

A golden age of satire has just ended. Say a fond farewell to some of the finest raw material satire has ever known: the worst president in American history, the worst political and economic ideas in American history, the worst political and economic policies in American history, the worst military and corporate corruption in American history, the worst governmental incompetence in American history, the worst constitutional abuses in American history, and the worst coverage of all the above by the worst news media in American history.

Sure enough, our intrepid satirists rose magnificently to the occasion. Who can forget late-night's ballsy takedowns of Republican evildoers like Paris Hilton, Jessica Simpson, Britney, Brangelina, Simon Cowell, Martha

Stewart, Jared the Subway Guy, Ozzie Osbourne, the cast of *The Hills*—in fact, of every reality show on earth? Or that brilliant parade of snarling, farting, balding, over-weight male stand-ups striding 24-7 across Comedy Central's stages, bringing malefactors to their knees? Can you name a satire of our health-care system as savage as *Scrubs*? Remember JibJab's slash-and-burn take on the '04 presidential race? Jesus, who can forget that? And c'mon, has there ever been a comedy star as fall-down-funny as Seth Rogen? OMG LOL.

Yeah, right.

It wasn't all bad. The liars, killers, and thieves in the White House insisted: "Satirize us and the terrorists win." Certain malcontents didn't listen. The stiletto-sharp, amazingly consistent Jon Stewart. Supersatirist Stephen Colbert, who displayed real courage when he puked all over the nice clean tux of a war criminal, to the huffy disapproval of the news media, who should've been doing the same thing. The edgiest and funniest women *SNL* has yet produced, Tina Fey and Amy Poehler. And let's hear it for the Irish: George Carlin kept up that White Harlem growl of furious dissent right to the end. Seth McFarlane's *Family Guy* did some of the best popular American satire since the onset of the American Millennium.

But there's always room for improvement. Some steps for recovery:

1. Humor's like surgery. It can be used to make rich people look less repulsive. Or it can be used to cure serious illness. Right now our system's seriously ill. Act accordingly.
2. The human sewage is finally out of power. Kick 'em while they're down. Make sure that even if they

escape the life-without-parole they deserve, they have to wear a laugh track for the rest of their natural lives.

3. Don't take your cues from TV news. It's wholly owned and operated by the folks who supported the aforementioned human sewage. Attack their puppets, but don't let them set your agenda.

4. If you ply your comedic trade on TV, don't do TV about TV. It might be hilarious, even devastating, but it's just more publicity for your targets. Ditto with celebrities.

5. Demand much, much better from the Internet. For the Second Coming of Media, it sucks comedy-wise. (But thank the God of Laff for *The Onion* and Andy Borowitz.)

6. Buy books, read books, write books, and publish or self-publish books. They remain the only major medium that's largely free of corporate censorship.

Step 6. Find a Sponsor

When you enter a recovery program, you must always remember that you are not alone. Many of us have been there. Many of us still are there. And many of us offer programs that can make your recovery much easier.

Recovery can save lives, but the process can be bumpy. Leaning on someone else can provide meaning and encouragement during those dark and lonely hours when you look around and realize that eight years of George W. Bush won't be undone in a short period of time.

Sponsors can help you find relief and keep you on the road to recovery during those tough times. They are supportive links to sanity, people who understand what you are going through, people who can help you mend your soul.

Selecting a sponsor is a very personal decision. Make sure your sponsor can offer you exactly what you need—not what you think another person would need, and not what you think you *should* need. Whomever you choose, own your decision.

Sponsors have generally been through exactly what you have. In fact, there's a saying in many 12-step programs: If you want what we have, you do what we did. The sponsor should offer the kind of support you want and be good at it because he or she has been through the program already.

By the way, there is nothing wrong with picking multiple sponsors. In fact, when you are recovering from eight years of Bush, the more sponsors you select, the more likely it is that recovery will happen for all of us across the country.

Here is a list of organizations that potentially can help you successfully navigate your way through recovery.

MoveOn.org (www.moveon.org)

This group was started in 1998 by Joan Blades and Wes Boyd, two Silicon Valley entrepreneurs who shared a deep frustration with the partisan warfare in Washington, D.C., and especially the wasteful spectacle of the Clinton impeachment. Now, with over 3.3 million members across the country, MoveOn.org works to realize the progressive vision of our country's founding fathers. You can become directly involved in the political process by keeping up with a slew of current campaigns, making donations, or signing petitions that go directly to the source—including Congress and the media.

People For the American Way (www.pfaw.org)

What better way to wrestle free from your addiction than a one-stop-shopping website for those hoping to fight domestic spying, ban torture, and stop the war in Iraq, all while supporting civil liberties and equal rights for all?

PFAW was founded in 1981 by Norman Lear, Barbara

MY HUSBAND WORKS VERY LONG HOURS, MY CHIL-DREN ARE AWAY AT SCHOOL, AND MY DOGS SPEND MOST OF THEIR DAY IN THE NEIGHBOR'S YARD. IF THEY WERE ALL AROUND, PERHAPS I WOULD BE MORE IN TOUCH WITH THE WORLD, AND WITH THIS COUNTRY. SO IT'S NOT MY FAULT THAT I AM LIVING IN COMPLETE DENIAL. WHERE ELSE CAN I LIVE? IT'S ALL THEIR FAULT.

Many people believe, as you do, that their failures are the fault of other people and animals rather than themselves. But think about it. Who is the one who pretends that the environment is in good shape? Who is the one who watches Bush's press conferences without a whimper? Who is the one who allowed this administration to get away with all its blunders? The truth is that if you entered recovery, you might find that your loved ones would be willing to spend more time around you, especially your dogs (who, history tells us, tend to vote Democratic).

Jordan, Father Theodore Hesburgh, and Andrew Heiskell to counter the growing clout of the radical right, and especially of televangelists such as Jerry Falwell and Pat Robertson. Since then, its television ads have influenced public opinion on a variety of political and social issues, helping to block the appointment of Robert Bork to the Supreme Court and oppose the right-wing Christian Coalition. PFAW continues to be an essential resource for communicating with local legislators and media outlets.

The Democratic Party (www.democrats.org)

The Democratic Party was founded in 1792 by Thomas Jefferson as a way to fight the "elitist" Federalist Party. It is the party that has been most associated with the battles for women's suffrage, progressive income tax, labor rights, child welfare laws, and civil rights. Its mission hasn't changed, nor have its values of wisdom and compassion over wealth and social status. In addition to Jefferson, previous Democratic leaders include John Quincy Adams, James Madison, William Jennings Bryan, Franklin Roosevelt, John F. Kennedy, and Bill Clinton. A former chairman of the party, Ron Brown, said, "The common thread of Democratic history . . . has been an abiding faith in the judgment of hardworking American families, and a commitment to helping the excluded, the disenfranchised and the poor strengthen our nation by earning themselves a piece of the American Dream. We remember that this great land was sculpted by immigrants and slaves, their children and grandchildren."

Habitat for Humanity (www.habitat.org)

Millard and Linda Fuller founded Habitat for Humanity in 1976; it has grown into a worldwide Christian housing ministry striving to ensure that all people have a place to live in dignity and safety. While ostensibly Christian, it is dedicated to its mission as an ecumenical nonprofit organization. All who desire to be a part of the organization are welcome to help in the fight to eliminate substandard housing and homelessness.

The Fullers were a wealthy business couple before founding the organization; a reevaluation of their lives led them to sell all of their possessions, give the money to the poor, and search for a new focus. They ended up in a Christian community in Georgia and there created the idea for a ministry based on building houses for low-income families that the families could afford. The houses are built almost entirely by volunteers with varying degrees of skill, and the work is supervised by trained staff. Habitat for Humanity gives the owner a no-interest loan in order to make the home affordable.

Sierra Club (www.sierraclub.org)

The Sierra Club is America's oldest, largest, and most influential grassroots environmental organization, with more than 750,000 members who work to protect the environment. The club has been tenacious in its criticism of the Bush administration's giveaways to big energy companies, also known as the Energy Task Force. Bringing light to the fact that the task force was composed of behemoths like ExxonMobil, which wrote the resulting national energy policy, the Sierra Club fought all the way to the Supreme Court. Through the club's vast network dedicated to congressional lobbying and grassroots action, members have the opportunity to get involved with local chapters, be part of a national network of environmental advocates, and gain the satisfac-

WHEN CHILDREN ARE REPUBLICAN

Sometimes, despite our best efforts as parents, children go astray. They can fall into temptations such as alcohol, drugs, and/or Republicanism. When they succumb to the latter, you must show patience. Your children may simply be acting out their anger or other negative emotions toward you. They are not really Republicans. They are just asking for your love and attention.

It is true, however, that when a parent has an issue, the child is seven times more likely to develop that same problem. This is why it is so important that you enter recovery, and stay recovered. You cannot Republican-proof your child, but you can set a loving example.

tion of helping preserve irreplaceable wild lands and wildlife.

The Carter Center (www.cartercenter.org)

Based in Atlanta, Georgia, and founded in 1982 by President Jimmy Carter and his wife, Rosalynn, this organization has been working to improve the quality of human life and human rights domestically as well as around the world for more than twenty-five years.

Through their work at the center, the Carters have been instrumental in aiding African countries to increase agricultural production, raise awareness of preventive medicine in Africa as well as in Latin America, and help prevent civil and international conflicts throughout the world.

Doctors Without Borders (www.doctorswithoutborders.org)

This organization is composed of doctors and other medical personnel who venture into areas of armed conflict, epidemics, natural disasters, and anywhere medical humanitarian aid is needed to assist people whose survival is threatened by violence, neglect, or catastrophe. Created in 1971 by French doctors and journalists (its official name is Médecins sans Frontières), it remains neutral in the face of any political disputes in the areas it serves, its only mission being to render care on the basis of need. In the past twenty years, the doctors have worked with the victims of the Rwandan genocide, the Serbian massacre, the crisis in Darfur, and the conflicts involving civilian targeting in Africa.

MAKING YOUR HOME A RECOVERY ZONE

You've worked hard on your recovery. You are living the good life, free of bad speeches, poor diplomacy, and ill-timed wars. Do not allow the same mechanisms that lured you into your problem in the first place to fester in your home. Thus, make sure that you:

- Keep no Bush memorabilia in your home. Let your whole family know that you are in recovery, and ask them for your support. Your children may think it's funny to make pro-Bush statements or act like George W. Bush at a party, but you must let them know this is not acceptable behavior.
- Explain to your family why your home is a Bush-free one. "Our family is not like other families," you can say. "We are in recovery. They are still stuck in the early 2000s."
- Don't turn on the radio except to listen to music. If you hear the voice of Rush Limbaugh, you are tempting fate. If you *want* to hear the voice of Rush Limbaugh, you are in danger of relapse and need to enter an intense recovery program now.
- Be suspicious of the mainstream media, especially the Associated Press's political coverage, which slants far to the right.
- Never watch Fox News.

American Civil Liberties Union (www.aclu.org)

The ACLU, founded in 1920 by Roger Baldwin, Crystal Eastman, and Albert DeSilver, among others, is a nonprofit, nonpartisan group that has grown from being a roomful of civil liberties activists to an organization of more than four hundred thousand members and supporters. The ACLU has litigated against many of the Bush administration's trademark policies, including trampling of constitutional rights by the Patriot Act, the denial of due process for detainees and their abuse at Guantanamo, and the illegal and blatantly unconstitutional surveillance of U.S. citizens without warrant by the National Security Agency. There's an ACLU affiliate in every state and Puerto Rico that handles requests for legal assistance, lobbies the state legislatures, and hosts public forums throughout the year.

MUSIC

John Hartmann began his professional career in the mail room of the William Morris Agency, where he later served as office liaison to Colonel Tom Parker, Elvis Presley's manager. A veteran music agent, personal manager, and record executive, he has provided career direction for Sonny & Cher; Buffalo Springfield; Neil Young; Joni Mitchell; the Eagles; Peter, Paul & Mary; Crosby, Stills & Nash; Jackson Browne; America; and many others. He is also the founder and CEO of HolodigmMusic.com, an online training system for musicians and entrepreneurs, and lectures at Loyola Marymount University, where the students voted him outstanding professor in 2007 and 2008.

The last line of defense in any democracy is the arts. The wandering minstrels of ancient China, the troubadours of medieval Europe, and American folk heroes like Woody Guthrie all embraced the tradition of speaking truth through the power of song.

Woody reminded us of our obligation to seek peace and demand justice for ourselves and each other. He inspired a generation of folksingers to stand up and protest, perhaps the most eloquent of those being Pete Seeger, whose songs became the foundation of the modern folk movement, including "We Shall Overcome," the undisputed anthem of the civil rights movement.

When Bob Dylan embraced the electric guitar, he launched the Folk Rock era: The Beatles; Buffalo Springfield; Crosby, Stills, Nash & Young; and most of their contemporaries followed suit. It can be argued that music precipitated the end of the Vietnam tragedy. John Lennon left us to "Imagine" the possibilities.

But the military-industrial monster has never left us, and today there is little to no political recourse, because the musicians have been silenced. Many, blinded by propaganda, have abdicated their obligation to serve the truth. Those who do sing out face a vicious backlash. In 2003 the Dixie Chicks' Natalie Maines declared, "I just want you to know we're ashamed the president of the United States is from Texas." The group's records were then banned from country radio, and the dangers inherent in radio station owner Clear Channel's control of the airwaves became clear.

Other artists, great and small, have challenged the reckless direction of the Bush administration. Neil Young, Jackson Browne, Nine Inch Nails, and many others have protested. But their message has been concealed behind the corporate veil.

The truth is young and lives in the street. So next time you see a ragged musician singing on the corner, stop and listen. Give him your time, and drop a dollar in his jar. And if I may fuse an analogy from Harrison and Hemingway, ask not why his guitar gently weeps; it weeps for you.

Help musicians recover their power.

1. Dissolve the myth that monolithic corporate media are liberal. When programming describing itself as the purveyor of "news" is attached to the appellation "show," trust that something is wrong. Big business owns the media.
2. Work to break up the corporate media monopolies. The regulations that once precluded individual companies from owning and operating more than seven

television stations should be restored. The control of radio stations and newspapers should be adjusted similarly.

3. Take the profit out of the electoral system. The broadcast airwaves belong to the people. Radio and television should be required, as part of their licensing mandate, to provide free airtime to qualified candidates seeking public office.

4. Demand funding for music programs in elementary schools. Musical talent is lying dormant in the hearts and minds of a generation of young people. Much of it goes undiscovered because of a lack of music education in public schools.

5. Inspire young people to question authority and seek the truth. When propaganda programming and pseudo-patriotism create fear in the populace, there is no breeding ground for protest.

Step 7. Remember the Terrible Things That Have Happened

You've come a long way in your recovery, but now it's time for what might be the hardest, grittiest part of the process: taking inventory.

In the early stages of recovery, most people are still foundering in some state of denial. They know their problem exists, but they're still not quite ready to admit all the terrors of their recent past. Their egos won't let them admit that terrible incidents may have taken place—things that wouldn't have had to happen if recovery had come sooner.

It's time to give your ego a real shock—perhaps the very shock that will jerk you out of your haze. It's time to face the painful truth and take a close, unflinching look at the damage wrought by George W. Bush and the power he held over you.

Perhaps the most destructive result of the George W. Bush–induced haze was the Iraq war. New evidence uncovered by Pulitzer Prize–winning journalist Ron Suskind shows that not only were George W. Bush and his staff aware that Iraq did not possess weapons of mass destruction, they fabricated evidence to make it look as if it did. But even setting aside its false justification, the eventual war was thoroughly botched by underequipping troops, leaving Iraqi weapons depots unguarded, disbanding the Iraqi army, and abandoning wounded U.S. soldiers in the squalor of Walter Reed Army Medical Center. Mistake after mistake turned Dick Cheney's fantasy that we would be "greeted as liberators" into a nightmare. As of August 2008, 4,141 American soldiers had been killed and 30,324 injured, along with more than 94,490 Iraqi civilians killed.

The war's financial toll has also been staggering: A total of $600 billion has been spent, with an additional $400 million spent each day it continues.

The war's psychological toll has been equally devastating. The United States has been blamed for the deaths of thousands of innocent civilians, fanning anti-American sentiment. And the constant redeployment duties for American soldiers serving in Iraq have taxed morale—more than 45 percent say it is low or very low—and strained America's military resources. The Pentagon itself has said that there is a "significant" risk that the military cannot quickly and fully respond if it is needed elsewhere in the world.

Ironically, the Iraq debacle has distracted America from its stated goal of making the nation safer in its battle against terrorists. Experts agree universally that Afghanistan is the most important military front in this fight. The Taliban is rebuilding, Afghanistan's border with Pakistan remains outside the rule of any recognized law, and

Osama bin Laden is still thought to be operating there. But the U.S. military, mired in Iraq, has been unable to devote the resources needed to secure Afghanistan.

Another devastating casualty of the Iraq war is America's moral leadership. Photos of abuse in Abu Ghraib, tales of humiliation at Guantanamo, reports of kidnapping and torture in secret CIA locations—all of these have destroyed the faith and goodwill America earned over decades of working hard to establish and operate by international agreements such as the Geneva conventions.

On the domestic front, annihilating long-trusted American institutions commanded the administration's highest attention. The government's failure to act after Hurricane Katrina devastated New Orleans proved that it was no longer able to conduct its fundamental duty of assisting its people and cities in times of natural disaster. Nobody at the Federal Emergency Management Agency (FEMA)—the people who are supposed to lead such rescue efforts—grasped the magnitude of the crisis. Three years later, only 72 percent of the city's population has returned, sixty-five thousand properties remain blighted, a fraction of the funds that George W. Bush promised have been delivered, and Secretary of Homeland Security Michael Chertoff, to whom FEMA reported during and after Katrina, still has his job.

Bush's demolition of American institutions penetrated every aspect of government. The Environmental Protection Agency let its pursuit of criminal prosecutions against polluters drop by one-third, and it refused to enforce certain laws under the Clean Air Act until it was successfully sued before the Supreme Court. The Department of Labor, after spending most of the eight Bush years cutting budgets for primary activities such as enforcing occupational safety and health regulations as well as minimum wage and child labor laws, worked frantically in its final months to water down those same laws. George W. Bush's No Child Left Behind legislation imposed new testing requirements on public schools but gave no additional money to enforce these requirements, putting great strain on these schools. Then he increased the funding and tax breaks for private and parochial schools because "parents should be able to take the federal money attributable to their child . . . and make a choice of any school they want to send that child to."

George W. Bush reworked Medicare, which was launched in 1965 to provide medical coverage for the nation's elderly, in a scheme that is costing taxpayers $1.2 trillion over its first ten years. Some users are being charged as much as $3,850 a year in prescription fees, while drug company profits are protected as the companies make top dollar from drugs purchased through the program.

American government was once stocked with the best and the brightest people. During the past eight years, these public servants were pushed aside to make room for ideologues and cronies. Once again, the Iraq war provides the most glaring example: The Army's chief of staff, General Eric Shinseki, was forced to retire because he challenged former Secretary of Defense Donald Rumsfeld's disastrous assumption that Iraq could be invaded and controlled with less than "several hundred thousand soldiers." Former FEMA head Michael Brown possessed no job qualifications other than having worked on George W. Bush's 2000 election campaign, as opposed to the pre-Bush FEMA director, who had five years' experience as a statewide emergency services director and ten years as a judge.

George W. Bush's choice for the nation's chief medical officer, the surgeon general, was Dr. James W. Holsinger, Jr., who authored a white paper for the United Methodist Church on the biological reasons why homosexuality violates Christian teaching. The George W. Bush choice for American ambassador to the United Nations was John Bolton, who openly scorned the place. And even after the complete failure of the Iraq war, Bush appointed one of its chief architects, Paul Wolfowitz, to head the World Bank. Alberto Gonzales, Bush's choice for attorney general, the nation's top law enforcement official, instructed his staff to appoint only attorneys who would be loyal to Bush's political agenda, thus ending centuries of impartiality.

George W. Bush's two appointments to the Supreme Court, John Roberts and Samuel Alito, claimed during their Senate hearings that they would respect the principle of stare decisis, which says that judicial precedents will be permitted to remain. Instead, both of these appointees have gone on to side almost exclusively with the court's extreme conservatives, Antonin Scalia and Clarence Thomas, and reverse precedent in a number of cases.

The effect of George W. Bush wasn't felt only by Americans. He killed any hope of the country's participation in the Kyoto Protocol, an international accord on climate change. He ended America's participation in the Treaty on Non-Proliferation of Nuclear Weapons, nixed participation in the International Criminal Court, and effectively shut down stem cell research efforts because they conflicted with his particular take on Christian values.

In fact, permitting religion into areas of government that the Constitution generally discourages was a favorite tactic, whether it was reassigning social service and educational duties away from government agencies to churches, forcing the removal of anything but "abstinence only" messaging from all HIV/AIDS and teen pregnancy reduction efforts, or encouraging the inclusion of religious teaching, specifically intelligent design, in science curricula in schools.

Reviewing such lists of transgressions can be painful and may seem interminable, but in any recovery program, the full truth must be brought to light, which means at least a mention of energy policy. During all eight of his years in office, Bush never once promoted conservation. Dick Cheney's infamous energy policy meetings, which he still has not opened to public review, set the pace with industry-written passages on the new importance of coal and nuclear power in America's energy future—with all mentions of global warming excised and all support of renewable energy sources scrapped.

In sum, George W. Bush spent the last eight years doing as much as he could to diminish our faith in government. He did this by choking off funding so the government couldn't operate effectively, by putting people in charge who disregarded stated missions and expert knowledge about those missions, and by changing those missions to align with his narrow agenda, which usually served the wishes of large corporate interests.

All this was accomplished with your help. Your Bush-induced haze enabled these things to take place. To comprehend how this happened is part of the 12-step program. To remedy it is also part of the program, as you will soon see.

HAPPINESS BREAK

Before going to the next step, take a moment to refresh your soul. You have come far. You have far to go. Here are some suggestions for this stage in your recovery:
- Open a door for a liberal.
- Wave to a Prius.
- Enjoy French cheeses.
- Take a solar hot water shower.
- Take a sailboat ride and let the wind be your power.
- Take a spa vacation in a rain forest.
- Lounge in a chair made out of recycled plastic.
- Make love in a house with an affordable mortgage.
- Watch children grow up in a better world.

OIL

Gregory Greene is a Toronto-based filmmaker whose highly influential 2004 documentary, The End of Suburbia, *forever changed America's conversation about oil and has become the informational tool of choice for the growing peak oil movement, comprising a wide range of industry professionals, NGOs, and citizen groups spanning the political spectrum. His most recent project,* Escape from Suburbia, *continues to examine the peak oil movement's controversial call to economic "relocalisation" and is presently on Canadian and U.S. television—and in indie theaters and living rooms around the world.*

Oil has driven America's economic growth for over one hundred years. This country was the world's greatest producer of oil until the 1970s, and oil has been so plentiful and cheap that we have built an entire way of life around it. Much of what we create or consume relies on petroleum, from toothpaste to iPhones, and the cars, trucks, and buses of our transportation fleet are entirely dependent on it.

The problem is that the American Way of Life is actually based on *cheap* oil—and the era of cheap oil is over. World oil production has been reaching its geophysical limits as old supergiant fields from the North Sea to the Arabian peninsula have reached the geological peak production.

"Peak" oil is not a difficult concept to understand. Oil production follows a bell curve and is subject to the laws of both thermodynamics and common sense: What goes up must come down. World oil production is currently reaching the top of that bell curve. In the coming years, we will all be riding its downward slide.

As George W. Bush himself has said, America is addicted to oil. And with world production declining and prices spiraling ever upward in the coming years, this addiction is going to be painful to break. But break our addiction to oil we must, for the sake of America's need for economic recovery and its future leadership of a sustainable global civilization.

Here are some suggestions for recovery from oil addiction:

1. Take some time to read a book or watch a movie about peak oil. Thinking about all the ways your life is connected to cheap oil, from how much gas you use to what kind of food you eat, will help you get a sense of how to reduce your dependence.
2. Get used to living with oil you can't afford. Reduce the size and the use of your car. Organize car sharing at work or take mass transit if it's available.
3. Eat locally grown food. Not only does it reduce your dependency on fossil fuels for transport, but it is an important way to reduce your carbon footprint.
4. Because we need real leadership to create real energy policies, we must hold our elected representatives to a higher standard than we have in the past. America needs a commitment to an energy policy as brave and far-reaching as the Apollo space program. This means making tough choices, such as ending subsidies to companies that produce fossil fuels and committing to decentralized energy sources and conservation.

This also means resuscitating America's moribund national rail and local public transit systems.

5. Apply pressure at the local level. As energy shortages and soaring prices force profound changes in the way we live, we will need to strengthen our communities and rebuild our economies. Getting involved in local institutions and organizations is challenging, but civic responsibility is the price of democracy. In the difficult times ahead, successful communities will have involved citizen groups working with local government, finding post-carbon solutions to the energy crisis with distributed local power sources, growing food, and creating green jobs.

6. Members of Congress have been advocating these solutions for years—the leader of the bipartisan Peak Oil Caucus is a Republican named Roscoe Bartlett. Read all about his efforts online and get involved with your local peak oil group. If there isn't one in your community, start one.

Step 8. Consider the People Whose Lives Have Been Harmed

The next crucial and painful step toward recovery is acknowledging the many people you have hurt by allowing George W. Bush to have power over you.

In order to emerge from your eight-year funk, you are going to have go deeper into the haze, walk back into that fog. You can't change until you become aware of all the people who have suffered by your choices and what happened to them. You cannot alter what happened, but you can learn from it. The past is the greatest teacher of all.

The number of people who could be included on this list is approximately several billion. Here are just a few of them:

1. Valerie Plame was an undercover CIA agent whose cover was blown by White House officials in their effort to harm her husband, Ambassador Joseph Wilson, who had publicly spoken out against Bush's Iraq invasion.

While Vice President Dick Cheney's chief of staff, Lewis "Scooter" Libby, was eventually convicted in relation to the leaking of Plame's identity to the press, the grand jury investigation in the case showed that Bush's right hand, Karl Rove, and possibly even Bush and Cheney themselves, played roles in outing her.

Cheney was incensed when Wilson, in a July 6, 2003, *New York Times* opinion piece, wrote that the "uranium yellow cake" President Bush had referred to as evidence of Iraqi weapons of mass destruction didn't exist. A plan was then hatched to reveal via a press leak that Plame worked undercover for the CIA; the leak appeared in Robert Novak's July 14, 2003, syndicated column. This leak endangered both Plame and other agents who were undercover at the time, and it effectively ended Plame's CIA career.

The ensuing investigation into the leak was a three-and-a-half-year-long chase. Bush-appointed U.S. attorney Patrick Fitzgerald was chosen as special prosecutor for the case. In a court filing he wrote:

> [Libby's] participation in a critical conversation with [*New York Times* reporter] Judith Miller on July 8 . . . occurred only after the vice president advised [Libby] that the president specifically had authorized [Libby] to disclose certain information in the National Intelligence Estimate.
>
> Libby testified that the circumstances of his conversation with reporter Miller (getting approval from the president through the vice president to discuss material that would be

classified but for that approval) were unique in his recollection.

Libby was sentenced to thirty months in prison and a $250,000 fine, but Bush commuted the prison sentence. Plame and her husband are currently pursuing a civil lawsuit against Cheney and other officials involved.

2. Brandon Mayfield, a native of Oregon and a lawyer, was a convert to Islam who had volunteered to defend some local Muslims accused of collaborating with terrorists. He was arrested by the FBI while leaving his home on May 6, 2004, and wasn't heard from again until the FBI was forced to release him two weeks later.

The FBI later claimed he had been arrested in connection with terrorist attacks in Madrid earlier that year. Using the U.S.A. Patriot Act as its justification, the FBI had tapped Mayfield's phones, accessed his bank records, and broken into his home to collect evidence.

When they finally arrested Mayfield, they held him without access to legal representation or communication with his family, and they wouldn't tell his family where or why he was being held.

After two weeks, Spanish authorities, announcing that they had their own suspects in the attacks, said they had contacted the FBI to inform them that Mayfield was the wrong person, but the FBI had ignored this information. Eventually Mayfield sued the FBI and the U.S. government and was awarded $2 million—and provisions of the Patriot Act were overturned on the basis of being unconstitutional.

3. At the age of twenty-six, Michael Schiavo's wife, Terri, collapsed in her apartment in Florida. When she was found, she wasn't breathing and had no pulse, and because too much time passed before she was resuscitated, she suffered severe brain damage. After months in and out of a coma, she was placed on a feeding tube and declared to be in a persistent vegetative state, with little to no chance for recovery.

Nonetheless, Schiavo made numerous attempts to spark recovery of his wife's brain, including providing experimental treatments and specialized facilities and obtaining certification for himself as an emergency room nurse and respiratory therapist.

After three fruitless years, and in consultation with his wife's physician, Schiavo halted most therapy and entered a Do Not Resuscitate order for Terri. Five years later he ceded control of his wife to the Pinellas County Circuit Court, which determined that she would not have wished to continue life-prolonging measures in such a situation. But Terri's parents, devout Roman Catholics, protested, and thus began a seven-year nightmare for Schiavo that saw his reputation as a loving husband smeared and his wife's wishes for a peaceful death ignored.

In 2003, Terri's parents retained antiabortion activist Randall Terry to raise the profile of their daughter's case and succeeded in turning it into a proxy fight in the war against abortion. By the time Terri Schiavo finally died on March 31, 2005, she had been the object of fourteen appeals in Florida courts, five suits in federal court, state legislation that was struck down by the Florida Supreme Court, a subpoena by a U.S. congressional committee trying to qualify her for witness protection, federal legislation, and four denials by the U.S. Supreme Court.

A most apt postscript to the entire fiasco was a line from a leaked memo by a political strategist for Florida Republican senator Mel Martinez calling the incident "a great political issue" for the Republicans.

4. Democratic senator Max Cleland of Georgia received two medals of valor in the Vietnam war, service that cost him three limbs. But this didn't stop George W. Bush's political henchmen from smearing Cleland as unpatriotic.

Cleland, whose legs and right arm were blown off by a grenade, returned to the United States and became an outspoken advocate for veterans. He served as the administrator of the Veterans Administration from 1977 to 1981, then as the secretary of state of Georgia from 1982 to 1996, before becoming a U.S. senator in 1996.

Unfortunately for Cleland, he was up for reelection in 2002, the year Karl Rove declared he'd stop at nothing to secure a Republican majority in the Senate. The Republicans put relatively unknown congressman Saxby Chambliss up against Cleland, and in a move that foreshadowed the swiftboating of John Kerry in 2004, ran a television ad calling into question Cleland's commitment to American homeland security and showing images of Saddam Hussein and Osama bin Laden along with those of Cleland.

The ad received immediate condemnation, most notably from Republican senators and fellow Vietnam veterans John McCain and Chuck Hagel, who forced its removal. But the damage had been done,

AFFIRMATIONS

Affirmations are positive statements you say aloud or to yourself that help you feel comfortable with the changes you want to make in your life. Memorize and then repeat them as often as you wish. The more you do, the more likely it is that they will come true.

Today I accept that George W. Bush is no longer president.

I am entering a new and blessed phase of my time on earth.

The worst day after January 20, 2009, will be better than any of the 2,922 days before it.

Tomorrow is the first day of the rest of my life without George W. Bush as president.

I believe in a power greater than myself: the U.S. Constitution.

I trust the Constitution to guide me through all legal and political conundrums.

Because my life is free of George W. Bush, my days are filled with joy and wonder.

and Cleland lost his reelection bid. He has since spent much of his time working to oppose George W. Bush and his policies.

Alongside the individuals cited previously as having suffered damage during the Bush years are countless others. George W. Bush's war on Iraq has killed tens of thousands of Iraqis and has turned the country of Iraq into a war zone. In addition, more than four thousand Americans have been killed there, and a 2008 report in *The New England Journal of Medicine* estimates that more than 135,000 soldiers returning from Iraq suffer from post-traumatic stress disorder and will deal with its effects for the rest of their lives.

Other victims of the Iraq debacle are the Iraqis who were tortured, humiliated, and in some cases killed at Abu Ghraib and similar places. Likewise, in other American detention centers around the world, legitimate suspects and others erroneously detained have been subjected to degradation and abuse.

Within the United States, there are the victims of Hurricane Katrina: Not only did 1,577 lose their lives and over one million their homes, but the region has never recovered from the rescue George W. Bush botched and then ignored.

Then there are the forty-seven million Americans living without any health insurance or regular health coverage. Forty-four million elderly people now pay more for Medicare thanks to George W. Bush's changes to the program, and an estimated forty-three million are living with substandard treatment even though they have insurance.

George W. Bush's economic and labor policies mean there are more than twelve million working poor in this

AS A LIFETIME LIBERAL, I AM ASHAMED TO ADMIT
THAT I WENT INTO AN EIGHT-YEAR FOG AND
DIDN'T LIFT A FINGER TO HELP THIS COUNTRY. I AM
SO EMBARRASSED THAT I AM IMMOBILIZED. NOW I
WANT TO JOIN A WORTHY ORGANIZATION, BUT I AM
AFRAID TO DO SO FOR FEAR THAT THE OTHER MEM-
BERS WILL LAUGH AT ME.

*Like that of someone who contracts a sexually transmitted
disease but is too ashamed to admit it to a doctor, your attitude will
only lead to further degradation. The more you shrink from your
problem, the worse off you will be. Instead, join a Bush Recovery
Group, where you will find many others like yourself. This will give
you a good opportunity to make fun of them, taking the heat off of
you.*

country—even though they possess paying jobs, they are not living above the poverty line. Thirteen million Americans are working at jobs that pay a minimum wage, a wage George W. Bush fought hard to keep unchanged during his eight years (and ultimately lost, thanks to the Democrats).

Because George W. Bush has refused to exercise necessary regulation over business and finance, 750,000 families have lost their homes to foreclosure and more than 40,000 employees watched their retirement funding disappear in the collapse of companies such as Enron and WorldCom. All American taxpayers are picking up the cost for bailing out high-flying banks and financial institutions that not long ago were paying their management obscenely high bonuses. And every American is paying higher energy and food costs because George W. Bush has spent the last eight years engineering the American economy to be more rather than less dependent on fossil fuels.

It's safe to say that almost everyone in America has been hurt by George W. Bush and the power he held over us. Only by recognizing this destruction, and devoting ourselves to healing it, can we fully recover. Once we start this healing process, we grow, and this growth will ensure that we will never fall under his spell—and that of others like him—again.

STRESS

Mark Liponis, M.D., is the corporate medical director of Canyon Ranch, the world's leading health resort, and the bestselling author of Ultraprevention *(with Dr. Mark Hyman) and* Ultralongevity. *An expert and national spokesperson on prevention and well-being, he heads a multidisciplinary holistic health practice incorporating nutrition, fitness, and emotional and mental health. His next book,* Rhythmic Health, *will be published in 2010.*

You just don't seem to have the energy or stamina you had eight years ago. You're not sleeping as soundly. You've put on some weight; most of it is around your midsection.

Your blood pressure has crept up. You get terribly bloated after eating. You've developed an unhealthy relationship with sweets. Your cholesterol and triglyceride levels are up. You find yourself drinking coffee in the morning to get going and alcohol at night to wind down. Your self-esteem has gone into hiding.

Does any of this sound familiar?

Chances are that you've chalked up these changes to aging. Wait a minute! It's only been eight years! You actually may be suffering from a common affliction now affecting tens of millions of Americans: CPES, or Chronic Presidential Embarrassment Syndrome.

This common syndrome is caused by chronic release of fight-or-flight hormones cortisol and adrenaline. Research suggests that this may be partly to blame for the explosive rise in obesity, diabetes, and related disorders over the past eight years.

Although stress is difficult to quantify and each person reacts differently to it, one important measure is the gap between a person's expectations and reality. Frustration and unmet desires are a source of continual stress that has adverse health effects. This stress has been linked with cardiovascular disease, including high blood pressure and heart attack. Unhealthy coping mechanisms often involve eating disorders and substance abuse. Chronic stress has also been shown to affect fertility, sleep patterns, heart rhythm, memory, and a person's overall sense of well-being.

The good news is that there is help, and there are six steps you can take right now to start to ameliorate the symptoms of this common condition:

1. **Meditate.** Reducing levels of cortisol and adrenaline through meditation can be helpful. Choose a quiet, private space where you can sit comfortably. Pay attention to your breathing: in through your nose, out through your mouth. Repeat a mantra over and over in your mind—for example, "It's almost over, it's almost over," or "Two-term limit, two-term limit."
2. **Exercise.** Blowing off some steam while exercising is a great way to reduce stress and improve the symptoms of CPES. Try punching a punching bag or playing speedball. Martial arts help release tension and aggression. Jog around your neighborhood carrying a banner with your new favorite political candidates' names.
3. **Join a support group.** Look for a local group in your area, check online, or see Step 6 of this book.

4. **Get a massage.** Professional work on areas of muscle tightness and spasm in the neck, shoulders, and back can help relieve the pain associated with stress and CPES.

5. **Listen to music.** Listening to relaxing music can also help relieve stress and soothe your adrenal glands. Try Ben Harper's "Better Way," will.i.am's "Yes We Can," or Joss Stone's new campaign song.

6. **Empower yourself.** Learning that you do have some say in changing your situation is a critical step. The best way to feel self-empowered is to vote! You can also empower others to take the same critical step and help the millions of people suffering from CPES.

Step 9. Make Amends

Those last two steps were tough—very tough. Hearty congratulations for making it through them. You have turned a very important corner in your 12-step program. You have openly admitted your past. You have seen through your haze. You are now ready to take action. You are ready to make amends for the damage you coenabled.

The goal here isn't to make you feel better by alleviating any guilt you might be carrying. No, the goal is more real, more pragmatic: You can help repair some of the damage you have allowed to happen—to yourself and to the country.

Making amends is difficult indeed. But by doing so, not only will you clean up the mess you have made for yourself but, more important, you will help guarantee that no one else ever has to slog through that mess again.

Action 1: Get to Know the Constitution

You now recognize the Constitution as the higher power that should guide your actions. But how well do you actually know it? The good news is that it's an easy read—short and understandable. Read it; reread it; talk about it with friends and family; make it an integral part of your new life. Those who don't know the Constitution are doomed to forfeit its protections.

Action 2: Vote

How did George W. Bush get into office twice? Not enough people voted against him. In fact, 40 percent of eligible Americans didn't even bother to show up for the 2004 presidential election.

But presidential elections are just the tip of the iceberg. Much of Bush's eight-year reign of terror occurred because other elected officials didn't think you cared.

How do you show you care? You vote in every election, all the way down to the level of your local school board and city council seat. No matter how much a candidate spends on getting elected, there's still only one way he or she can win: by getting more votes than the other people running. (Unless they're George W. Bush, but that's another book.)

Before you vote, get to know the people who are running and familarize yourself with the issues they'll be dealing with. Demand satisfactory answers, and keep your copy of the Constitution handy. Then tell your friends, neighbors, and family what you've learned and get them to vote as well. In 2006, the average race for the House of Representatives cost $1.3 million per candidate. That equals about $15 per vote. So if you get ten of your friends and family members to vote for the better candidate, you just gave that candidate $150 worth of support. Vote as if your future depended on it. It does.

Action 3: Keep in Touch with Elected Officials

Whether or not your candidate wins, people are elected to represent you. But they can't do that unless you tell them what you think. Figure out the easiest way to communicate with them, whether by phone, letter, e-mail, fax, or, even better, in person when you see them walking down the aisle of your local market or at a public event.

Yes, it's hard to get their attention when lobbyists and other well-financed interests have their ear, which is all the more reason to keep after them. You can also join with other people like you to become members of or create your own well-financed interests to keep after them. If you're appalled by the use of torture, look to Amnesty International (amnestyusa.org). If you're concerned about civil rights, try the American Civil Liberties Union (aclu.org). If climate change is your focus, try Al Gore's WeCanSolveIt.org. These groups and many more, covering a broad range of important issues, can connect your energy—and your money—with other like-minded individuals so that your voices are heard; they know how to keep pressure on your elected officials, through lobbying, the courts, and public relations.

Action 4: Make Your Money Speak for You

It's great to write your elected representatives and lobby them through groups you support, but you're already speaking very loudly with the money you spend every day on food, clothing, transportation, and entertainment. If you're concerned about climate change, can you have a positive impact with the food you're buying? You bet. Each item of food has a carbon footprint based on how much carbon is released in its manufacture and shipment. A helpful website for learning about this is eatlowcarbon.org.

I ADMIT THAT I HAVE BEEN IN A REPUBLICAN-INDUCED STUPOR FOR EIGHT YEARS, BUT THIS ISN'T THE RIGHT MOMENT TO COME OUT OF IT. NEXT WEEK I AM GOING TO SIGN A DEAL WITH SOME TOXIC POLLUTERS WHO WANT TO USE MY VACATION PROPERTY AS A DUMP. I WILL MAKE A FORTUNE.

Okay, but what about the next big piece of business, and the next, and the next? When will you ever be able to draw a line in the sand and say enough is enough? If your doctor tells you to protect your skin against the sun, you start wearing sunscreen. If your dentist tells you that you have a cavity, you get it filled. Treat your stupor like any other medical emergency, and act now, not later.

ExxonMobil, which has slashed benefits for its employees and shirked its environmental responsibilities while making the largest profits in the history of the world, isn't the only place where you can fill up your tank. Different companies obtain their oil from different places using different methods. They treat their employees differently as well. If you're going to continue bankrolling big oil, you might as well give your money to the least despicable company. The Sierra Club has a great online tool that provides information: www.sierraclub.org/sierra/pickyourpoison/.

How about that favorite restaurant? Is the staff legal? Are they receiving fair wages and benefits? Your money may be playing out the undocumented-worker saga right in front of you. With every dollar you spend (or refuse to spend), you make a statement about changing the country's course.

Action 5: Become a Green Machine

Our planet needs recovery as much as you do; everything that happened to you happened to it as well.

Conservation is the easiest way to start. Any standard lightbulb in your home or office should be changed to an energy-saving compact fluorescent bulb. The new ones have improved light quality, and they last much longer than traditional bulbs. If every American home replaced just one standard bulb with a compact fluorescent one, enough energy would be saved to prevent the release of greenhouse gases equivalent to the emissions from more than eight hundred thousand cars a year.

Plug all of your various electronic devices, from computers to VCRs, in to power strips so you can easily turn them off when you aren't using them. Many of these devices still use power even when they're turned off, but the power strip lets you turn them off completely. Replace old, energy-intensive appliances, such as refrigerators, air conditioners, water heaters, and furnaces. In most cases you'll make back the cost in energy savings within the first year or two, and in some cases your local power utility will give you a rebate if you purchase appliances with Energy Star certification. Make sure your home is insulated properly. A small investment in insulation and window sealing will pay back almost immediately through energy savings.

Cut back on the amount of driving you do. Figure out a way to skip driving to work at least one day a week, by either carpooling, taking mass transit, or biking. When shopping, park in one central place and take the extra time to walk between destinations. Inflate your tires, which improves your gas mileage.

Beyond conservation, encourage the use of alternative, clean energy. As discussed earlier, the businesses you support with your consumer dollars make their own energy consumption decisions. Make sure you agree with them. Most power utilities let you choose the source of your electricity. These choices often include wind, solar, and hydroelectric. Tell them you want your source to be clean energy. It may cost a bit more, but you will have made a profound change in the environmental impact of your energy consumption.

Action 6: Go Back to School
This can mean attending continuing education classes or simply walking to your neighborhood school and asking if there's any way you can help out. All schools need help with tutoring, mentoring, and extracurriculars such as sports and the arts. Even attending community events like

sports matches, arts performances, or science fairs connects you to education and to future generations. Most people pay lip service to the important role education plays in our future, but hardly anybody sets foot in our communities' schools—and they need our help.

If getting to a school is out of the question, consider supporting a school—either one near you or one you attended as a child—with a donation of books or by sponsoring an extracurricular program. DonorsChoose.org does a great job of helping you do this.

Action 7: Spread the Health

Whether you're part of an HMO, participate in Medicare, or are one of the forty-seven million Americans without health insurance, the best protection against the skyrocketing health-care costs of the past eight years is to stay healthy, the best way to stay healthy is through prevention, and the best form of prevention is improved diet and more exercise.

And not only for you: Talk about it with friends, neighbors, and family. Start a walking group with your friends; share recipes that bring more fresh fruits and vegetables into daily meals; reconnect with old pals or relatives via an e-mail diet group. Make prevention a habit.

For more ideas, visit the U.S. Department of Health and Human Services diet and exercise website, smart-step.gov. Reach out to the elderly in your neighborhood who might need help getting the proper food or services they require to stay healthy. A short weekly visit by a neighbor can be just enough support to keep an elderly person living safely and comfortably in his or her own home.

Action 8: Be a Good Citizen

Although less tangible than the other suggestions, being a good citizen is what ties them all together. Recovery isn't simply about being sorry for the damage George W. Bush did. It's changing the way you interact with your community and our country so that someone like Bush can never damage us again. It means standing up for the Constitution and its values wherever and whenever you hear them being ignored—around the watercooler, on the soccer field, at a dinner party. It means caring about your values and being counted, whether by voting, signing petitions, donating money or time to a worthy cause, or standing with others to protest. It means recognizing the power that all of us have when we work together to correct the damage of the George W. Bush administration. This damage was created by people, and it can be fixed by people.

INTERNATIONAL IMAGE

Dubbed the "impresario of finance" by Institutional Investor *magazine, former Peace Corps volunteer Nathan Richardson has worked in Senegal, England, Poland, Turkey, Saudi Arabia, South Africa, and Liberia, where he led the International Rescue Committee's massive humanitarian relief effort. He also built Yahoo! Finance into the world's largest business news and finance outlet, and later became the head of Dow Jones online. He is currently CEO of ContentNext Media and publisher of paidContent.org., serves on the boards of LEAF and PlayNetworks, and is a technical advisor to MyC4, the Microfinance Information Exchange (MIX), and RGE Monitor.*

In 2003, two Bush acolytes in Congress made a push to whip up sentiment against the French by changing the word *French* to *freedom* in all things so named—including the now-famous "freedom fries." Novel, clever, but illogical and absurd.

Illogical and absurd international policy has, unfortunately, been key to the international Bush agenda, plunging the world's opinion of Americans to new lows; the United States is now viewed unfavorably by more than 60 percent of citizens in thirteen of thirty-seven countries polled, including most of the countries Bush is trying to democratize, as well as Spain, Germany, and France, three critical allies.

This came about as Bush set off on a foreign policy that included the disastrous war with Iraq, the loss of focus in a war in Afghanistan, mixed messages sent to

Georgia that helped provoke war with Russia, the failure to make progress in hot spots such as Israel and North Korea, and allowing the carnage in Darfur to continue.

However, by taking action we can save our reputation, not to mention the ability to maintain our standing on the world economic stage, and help other countries realize the democracy Bush promised.

How do we do this?

1. **Learn a language.** Only 9 percent of Americans are learning foreign languages, compared to 56 percent of Europeans. The more you can communicate, the better. Lobby for languages, as well. George W. Bush's education team cut language education from public schools at an alarming rate. Help reverse this.

2. **Get geographic.** Buy a world map. If you were born before 1975, you probably studied one that didn't include the breakup of the Eastern Bloc countries. The oil you consume may come from Kazakhstan; the flowers you buy, from Ecuador; the textiles for your clothing and household goods, from Mauritius; the raw material tantalum, used in your electronic devices, from Congo; the rice you eat, from Thailand. Keep in mind that we depend on other countries for our existence.

3. **Develop development.** With the world's population expected to grow by 25 percent in twenty years and 90 percent of the population living in the developing world, America's mandate to improve the lives of the world's majority will only intensify. The United Nations has become somewhat paralyzed, leaving the United States with a leading role in addressing the problem of the world's poor. Rather than take a fresh

look at the way we distribute taxpayer dollars, Bush layered the assistance machinery with new agencies, such as the President's Emergency Plan for AIDS Relief (PEPFAR) and the Millennium Challenge Corporation, and lumped USAID into the Department of State. Although Bush was right that development assistance is a diplomatic tool, the next president should follow the lead of other countries in creating a cabinet-level agency for development—truly leveraging our leadership, generosity, and desires to help turn the poor into a priority. Lobby your representatives to make this happen.

4. **Investments abroad are the new development and cold war.** China and India are gobbling up investment opportunities from the micro to the massive level around the world. American companies are hampered by 9/11-induced reporting requirements that make investing in foreign countries difficult. Unless we become aggressive in our strategic business investments abroad, we'll be hostage to the resource stranglehold of the Chinese and Indian companies. It is the new cold war, and we are losing by a long shot. Go online today, invest in emerging market mutual funds, find a micro-finance site such as www.myc4.com to promote small businesses, and realize that growth opportunities exist in these countries overflowing with comparative advantages.

5. **Go for one-on-one diplomacy.** If every American developed a good pen-pal relationship with someone in another country, we'd go a long way toward improving our understanding of the world and our image abroad—and we'd spend some quality time away from the television and computer.

Step 10. Avoid Relapse

Good for you! You've come a long way.

You're almost at that place where you can say proudly, "I have recognized that I have a problem, and I am well on the road to recovery."

But please don't expect the road to be smooth—this is a journey that never ends. You will encounter opportunities for relapse. Life is not an asphalt highway. It is a bumpy, unpaved country lane, like the kind you see in our country's crumbling infrastructure.

A relapse (which literally means "to fall again") is a common situation among people who have overcome an addiction to something.

Let's say you're at a party, and your glass falls off the table. Someone says, "I'm pretty sure that's an earthquake." As people around you leap into action, your response is the same one you had during all those years of Bush. You pay no attention. You do nothing. You may look shocked momentarily, but ultimately you just go back to reading the children's book you were holding.

These relapses are okay. They will happen. Experiencing a relapse does not mean that you are lost.

The most common time for a relapse to occur is just after recovery. So right now, be careful! You have made so much progress and have come so far; now you must remain vigilant.

It is important to be aware of situations that can trigger a relapse. Here is a sample list of such situations contributed by the many fellow travelers on the road to recovery.

- Renewing old friendships with Republicans
- Drinking O'Doul's and eating pretzels at the same time
- Thinking that the person you are having a beer with would make a good president, and therefore voting for him
- Your father getting you your first, second, third, and fourth jobs
- Shooting a friend in the face
- Making a friend apologize for letting you shoot him in the face
- Wearing a flight suit with a crotch bulge to work
- Attending the Olympics and, in front of three billion people, looking at your watch, bored; then, tapping the American flag on your knee
- Invading a neighbor's property because you are convinced he is hiding a bomb in his garage
- Taking the whole family on vacation to Kentucky's Creation Museum, where you take careful notes
- Asking Harriet Miers for legal advice
- Saying "Heckuva job," to people who are flailing
- Shooting a hocker on the White House lawn

- Shopping for a new car and pretending to look at hybrids, but then buying an SUV—because you need it for the dog
- Giving people odd nicknames, such as Kenny Boy, Poppy, Pooty Poot, Congressman Kick Ass, Wondergirl, Stretch, and Corndog

When you recognize or sense that any of these situations are arising, or they are rudely pointed out to you by other members of your recovery program, there are measures you can take:

- Go to Mount Rushmore and contemplate the good presidents.
- Keep a copy of the Constitution by your bed.
- Buy a Dixie Chicks CD and *do not* burn it.
- Listen to Miss South Carolina Teen USA answer a question at the Miss Teen USA competition and consider the importance of getting an education.
- Watch *The Colbert Report* on Comedy Central.
- Repeat all the steps you've already completed in your recovery program.
- Remember what it was like to live in the United States between the years 2000 and 2008. That should do the trick.

Here is a final thought before you move on to the next step: It is a given in all recovery programs that before you start to feel better, you will feel worse. What will that be like?

Well, you will start to recognize that you can't depend on a man in a flight suit to solve all your problems. You will feel desolate about the fact that your actions have con-

NINE-MONTHS-TO-LIVE FANTASY

Sometimes our problem is that we try to imagine the rest of our lives all at once—and we overextend ourselves, trying to do too much for too many people, possibly even failing to meet our own needs and wants. A useful way to counteract this problem is to think about your own death and what you would do if you knew you were going to die in nine months.

As he was dying, Republican advisor Lee Atwater (the Karl Rove of his time) said, "My illness helped me to see that what was missing in society is what was missing in me: a little heart, a lot of brotherhood. The 80s were about acquiring—acquiring wealth, power, prestige. I know. I acquired more wealth, power, and prestige than most. But you can acquire all you want and still feel empty. . . . It took a deadly illness to put me eye to eye with that truth, but it is a truth that the country, caught up in its ruthless ambitions and moral decay, can learn on my dime."

Maybe you would like to clean up the earth. Give a homeless person some money. Take a holiday by working at Habitat for Humanity. Gather crops at a sustainable farm. Discover someplace where you can find the little bit of heart that is missing in you. Never vote for a compassionate conservative again.

sequences. You will feel bad because you now know that polluting your local lake is a bad idea. You will sink lower knowing that going to war with every country you happen to dislike is not the answer to the world's problems. You will sink even lower when, instead of laughing at global warming, you acknowledge that it may indeed be a reality. You may hit rock bottom when you realize that every citizen of the United States is responsible for the election of the president. You can no longer deny what happened in the past.

The good news is that once you have hit rock bottom, you can't go any lower. From then on, it's all good news. Best of all, no matter what you do, no matter what happens in the world, George W. Bush will no longer be president.

James Gleick is one of America's most distinguished science writers. His bestselling books include Chaos: Making a New Science, *a National Book Award and Pulitzer Prize finalist that has been translated into more than twenty languages, and, most recently,* Isaac Newton. *He began his career as an editor and reporter for* The New York Times, *a position that he held for ten years, and he has written about science and technology for* The New Yorker, The Atlantic, The New Republic, *and other magazines. He is active on the boards of the Authors Guild and the Key West Literary Seminar.*

No one was actually burned at the stake, so you can't say the Bush administration was the worst in history for science. It was just the worst in the history of the American republic.

The problem began at the top, with an incurious, anti-intellectual, faith-based president who blithely disbelieved in evolution and global warming and who never tired of humiliating his own scientists with the same pathetic joke: "He's the Ph.D., and I'm the C student, but notice who's the advisor and who's the president."

Of all human endeavors, science is the one that's supposed to be dedicated to a neutral, dispassionate search for truth. That had no place in this most political of administrations. Career scientists were muzzled, research was suppressed, reports were censored. Political apparatchiks were put in charge of scientific review. If the subject was reproductive science or HIV prevention, abstinence was the only answer. If the subject was lead, mercury, atrazine, selenium, pesticides, no amount of scientific evidence could ever justify regulation. At the great scientific agencies—the National Center for Atmospheric Research, the Centers for Disease Control, the Environmental Protection Agency, and all the rest—careers were ended and morale plummeted.

Luckily the steps to recovery are clear:

1. **Put the scientists back in charge.** Experts aren't always right, but they're experts for a reason. Science is a profoundly self-correcting enterprise: Researchers who cheat, or fudge, or self-deceive seldom survive for long. The same can't be said of politicians.

2. **Let the light in.** The Bush administration drew the curtains shut and shoved unwanted research into desk drawers. The White House also did everything possible to keep its own deletions and revisions secret. No good. The products of government research must routinely be published, in journals or online. Internal debates, comments, criticism must all be open to public view.

3. **Keep private money out.** When interested parties pay for research, they get what they want. That goes for oil and coal companies studying climate change, pharmaceutical makers studying their own drugs, and everyone else.

4. **Take the muzzles off.** Government scientists must be free to take reporters' phone calls and to speak out wherever they want, not censored by politically run press offices.

5. **Reopen the borders.** The Bush administration interfered like none before with the travel of foreign scien-

tists to conferences and symposiums. It stifled overseas outreach by universities and technology companies. As the whole twentieth century showed, immigrants and refugees enrich American science immeasurably. Letting go of paranoia and xenophobia will make everyone feel better.

6. **Let the chips fall where they may.** When you ask for scientific research on a question—Do condoms prevent sexually transmitted disease? Are those aluminum tubes suitable for enriching uranium?—be ready to accept the answer, whatever it is.

Step 11. Carry the Message to Others

Step 11 is both challenging and exhilarating. It's your opportunity to use what you've learned so far to help people who are still struggling with addiction. As they say in 12-step programs, "In order to keep it, you have to give it away." In other words, service is an important part of recovery.

In fact, because you are in recovery, you know where to find others who have been similarly affected—you can probably pick them out in a crowd. After eight long years of experiencing rock bottoms, these souls need help. This is where you come in, armed with the tools and know-how to make a difference. You won't fall victim to the backslapping and clever nicknames again. Nor will you acquiesce when they invite you back to the ranch for jalapeño poppers and hot dogs. You're on a mission.

Every walk of a thousand miles begins with a single step, so before you do anything else, you've got to think about the places you can find Bush addicts. Think about your old haunts, and then think even bigger, someplace

I AM PRESENTLY WORKING IN AN ENVIRONMENT
WHERE I AM CERTAIN THAT EVERYONE ELSE IS A
REPUBLICAN. THEREFORE, I HAVE ONLY BEEN
ENGAGING IN THIS DEGRADING BEHAVIOR IN
ORDER TO EMULATE MY PEERS AND OBTAIN THEIR
ADMIRATION. HOW CAN I STOP WITHOUT INJUR-
ING MY RELATIONSHIP WITH THEM AND ENDAN-
GERING MY JOB?

*Your stationery reveals that you work for the Republican
National Committee. Get out now.*

more Texas-y and with more swagger. Think about the places where your addiction took root and then multiply them by 911. It's that bad.

It'll be a long, hard slog to reach these men and women. Here are some places to find them:

- **Toby Keith concert:** Country singer Toby Keith (born Toby Keith Covel) has been outspoken in his support of George W. Bush, and his fans love him for it. Log on to tobykeith.com and check the tour schedule. You will suffer through songs such as "Get Drunk and Be Somebody" and "Beer for My Horses," but keep in mind that almost everyone in attendance will need your help. Of course, to borrow from another of Keith's songs, they may also want to "put a boot up your ass," so dress accordingly.

- **NASCAR race:** In a similar vein, head down to your local NASCAR race. NASCAR is a sport in which the point is to drive around in circles, where drivers are punished for not staying the course, gas is consumed by the boatload, catastrophic wrecks are frequent, and fire suits are advised. It is essentially the automotive manifestation of the Bush administration.

- **NRA convention:** The National Rifle Association is a group of hearty guys and gals committed to protecting the American ideal of a gun in every home and a chicken hawk in every pot. The organization used to be led by the man best known for having played Moses in the movies, but when he retired, he turned the reins over to his trusty assistant, Wayne LaPierre.

- **Chuck E. Cheese:** Many of the most important decisions of the Bush administration were made at Chuck E. Cheese, and to this day it remains a popular hangout for neocons and Bush addicts. They're easy to spot. They're the ones in the pin-striped suits playing with the balls.

- **Oil companies:** With two oilmen in the White House, times have never been better for the industry. By 2008, gas prices were at an all-time high, every quarter saw ExxonMobil cranking out another record profit, and for eight years George W. Bush and Dick Cheney offered no real investment in alternative energy, no incentives to drive fuel-efficient cars, no ideas to conserve energy. The oil industry never had a friend like it did in those two. Withdrawal symptoms for these folks could be severe, so they may be receptive to your attempts to help them.

- **The U.S. Supreme Court:** Two of the approximately one hundred people in this country who found better jobs during the Bush administration currently sit on the Court. Bush appointed John Roberts and Samuel Alito to fill vacancies left by William Rehnquist and Sandra Day O'Connor, respectively, bringing even more Bush enthusiasm to the group that set aside the popular vote in 2000 and selected George W. Bush president to begin with. Both men fudged the truth during their confirmation hearings, so they might be feeling guilty and be ready to turn.

- **The New Haven Horseshoes Club:** No sport is synonymous with the Bush dynasty like horseshoes (other than, maybe, speed golf), and no location means more to the Bushes than George W.'s hometown, New Haven. The confluence of the two is a surefire place to find people who need help. If you hit enough of them on the head with a horseshoe, you might be able to knock some sense into them.

- **Britney Spears's house:** Not particularly known for her political stances, Ms. Spears did make one endorsement in 2004: She threw her considerable weight behind George W. Bush. Just one more addiction for Britney, who, at this point, is in dire need of help. Be forewarned: She may already be enrolled in many other 12-step programs.

- **The writing offices of late-night comedy shows:** For the past eight years, many people have borne the burden of the Bush presidency. For comedy writers, however, work was never easier. In an unusual display of outsourcing, writers simply hit Record on their TiVos, and George W. Bush did their job for them. From non sequiturs and malapropisms to gibberish, Bush was a walking, talking comedy highlight reel. These men and women will be in sorry shape. Help them.

- **Anyplace with five or more people:** Even in the darkest days of his presidency, George W. Bush enjoyed the support of at least 20 percent of Americans. Do the math. If you and four other people cram into a New York City taxicab, a roller coaster in Iowa, or a sweat lodge in New Mexico, chances are that one of you is still a Bush addict.

- **Wyoming:** The Cowboy State. The whole state. Seriously.

HISTORICAL RECOVERY

As philosopher George Santayana famously said, "Those who cannot remember the past are doomed to repeat it." And then there are those who do remember the past but aren't able to repeat it because times have changed. Laws have been passed. Society has new rules. People don't throw mummies into rivers anymore.

Here is a history lesson on how one group of people dealt with their recovery problem. Nineteenth-century German historian Ferdinand Gregorovius (as translated by Mrs. G. W. Hamilton) describes the fate of Pope Formosus (reign 891–896), who presided over a particularly contentious period of history:

> The corpse of the Pope [Formosus], taken from the grave where it had lain for eight months, and clad in pontifical vestments, was placed upon a throne in the council chambers. The advocate of Pope Stephen arose, and, turning to the ghastly mummy, beside which a trembling deacon stood as a counsel, brought forward the accusations; and the living Pope, in his insane fury, asked the dead: "Why hast thou in thy ambition usurped the Apostolic seat, thou who wast previously only Bishop of Portus?" The counsel of Formosus, if terror allowed him to speak, advanced no defense.

> The dead was judged and convicted; the Synod signed the act of his deposition, pronounced sentence of condemnation upon him, and decreed that all the clergy ordained by Fortunatus should be ordained anew. The Papal vestments were torn from the mummy, the three fingers of his right hand, with which the Latins bestowed the benediction, were cut off; with barbarous shrieks the dead man was dragged from the hall through the streets, and amid the rush of the yelling rabble was thrown into the Tiber.

GAYS AND LESBIANS

Christian minister, author, and filmmaker the Reverend Dr. Mel White ghostwrote books for fellow evangelicals, including Billy Graham, Pat Robertson, and Jerry Falwell. He came out as a gay man in 1993 and has since devoted himself full-time to ministering to lesbians, gays, bisexuals, and transgendered people. In 1997, the ACLU awarded him the National Civil Liberties Award for applying the "soul force" principles of Gandhi and Dr. Martin Luther King, Jr., to the struggle for justice for sexual minorities, and in 1998 he and his partner, Gary Nixon, founded Soulforce, an organization devoted to those efforts. White's two books are Stranger at the Gate: To Be Gay and Christian in America *and* Religion Gone Bad: Hidden Dangers of the Christian Right.

During the reign of George W. Bush, the power of fundamentalist Christians in American politics rose alarmingly, and the administration used religious leaders to mount a series of vicious political campaigns against lesbians and gays to raise hundreds of millions of dollars and to mobilize millions of votes.

In the presidential election of 2004, for example, the administration coordinated with antigay groups and churches to get anti–gay marriage initiatives on ballots across the country, ensuring large conservative voter turnout. Even after most of these initiatives passed, Bush worked closely with groups such as the Southern Baptist Convention, the Mormon Church, and the Catholic Church to push for a constitutional amendment against lesbian/gay marriage equality. This work against marriage equality, as well as similar efforts against adoption rights and employment nondiscrimination, stoked fear and hatred directed against lesbian, gay, bisexual, and transgendered (LGBT) Americans.

Such attacks created more than political damage for LGBT Americans; they damaged us spiritually. For most of us, the religion of our upbringing is a member of our family: sometimes like a nurturing aunt, often like a cranky uncle, but an integral part of our identity. And now we had to watch as that family member focused hatred against us, whether through Bush-engineered campaigns or continuing liturgical machinations, like the Pope's antigay pogroms or the Anglican church's antigay schism.

For most LGBT Americans, a recovery from eight brutal years of George W. Bush desperately calls out for a spiritual recovery as well. How to do it?

1. We realize that church leaders are dead wrong when they label homosexuality a sin to be forgiven and a sickness to be healed. The physical, psychological, historical, personal, and even biblical data show clearly that our sexuality is perfectly normal.

2. We quit supporting any religious institutions—just as most of us have with our political institutions—that aren't affirming of LGBT people.

3. We join faith communities that accept us without qualification, such as a Metropolitan Community Church or other welcoming and affirming congregations. Or we find new ways to develop our spirituality apart from religion. We can quit the churches of our childhood, but we must not quit our own spiritual journeys.

4. We spend as much time and money on developing our spirituality as we gay men spend on developing our pecs and abs. What is a strong body with a flabby soul?

5. We volunteer to help the less fortunate—otherwise our spirits shrivel and die. Imagine what would happen if we used our vast resources to mobilize against world hunger or mount a powerful campaign against the tragic spread of HIV/AIDS among our youth, especially our African-American and Hispanic youth.

6. We will recover from the past eight years of hyperbole and half-truths when we truly believe that our sexuality is a gift from God, and that it is to be accepted, celebrated, and lived with integrity; that we are loved by our Creator exactly as we were created; and that our spirits come to life when we are seeking justice and showing mercy to others. LGBT people were born to be spirit leaders. It would be a shame to waste our gifts.

Step 12. Say a Prayer

It is time to reach deep into your newfound commitment to your higher power and relish the warmth and support it provides. You have changed. You are not the person you were when you started these twelve steps. You have come a long way. You have become aware of your problem; you have helped others; you have made amends for your transgressions.

Most important, you will not let this happen again.

The final step is one that will remain with you, wherever your path takes you, for the rest of your life. It is a prayer that will be your friend, your inspiration, and your guide. It will reconnect you with the 12-step process that transformed you into what you are today.

The Political Serenity Prayer
Founding fathers grant me
The serenity to withstand the right wing
The courage to work for change
The wisdom to separate church and state

Living one day at a time
Voting in every election

Enjoying recycling and conserving our nation's
   resources, how precious they are
Accepting the phrase "we the people" to mean all
   the people, not just my people
Trusting the Constitution, in all its interpreta-
   tions, to provide clear direction on our road
   forward
Feeling powerful enough to prevent anyone,
   including my own government, from making
   me fearful
Knowing that this country may be reasonably
   well governed and prosper in its growth, during our lives and the lives of our children,
   and their children, and so on.
Amen

Sonja Lyubomirsky, Ph.D., author of the bestselling How of Happiness, *is a professor of psychology at the University of California, Riverside. Originally from Russia, she received her A.B., summa cum laude, from Harvard University and her Ph.D. in social/personality psychology from Stanford University. She currently teaches courses in social psychology and positive psychology and serves as the Department of Psychology's graduate advisor. She is an associate editor of* The Journal of Positive Psychology *and (with Ken Sheldon) holds a five-year grant from the National Institute of Mental Health to conduct research on the possibility of permanently increasing happiness.*

Bad stuff happens to all of us. The George W. Bush presidency is an example. Where to begin?

According to an August 2008 Associated Press poll, only 18 percent of those polled believed the country was on the right track; 76 percent felt it was on the wrong track. Six years before, 68 percent of the country felt it was on the right track. A July 2008 CNN opinion poll showed that only 3 percent of this country thought things were going "very well." And a poll taken by NBC in that same month found that only 13 percent liked the direction this country was taking.

People are not happy in America. How to recover?

1. Many psychological studies suggest that one of the most effective recovery methods is to recognize some benefit in having lived through those eight years. This

may be difficult, but thoughtful people have the ability to do it. Perhaps the Bush years led you to reorder your priorities, or to recognize strengths that you never thought you had, or to find a new purpose. Perhaps it prompted you to make new friends, to share humorous videos and stories, and to bond with others who share your views.

2. Sometimes it takes a bad event to shake things up, to compel paradigms to shift, to push our thinking to a higher level. As philosopher Friedrich Nietzsche wrote, "That which does not kill me makes me stronger." Granted, the W presidency may have produced a chain of events that led to many deaths, but it didn't kill most of us. Instead, perhaps it transformed us in ways that might make it better in the end.

3. Psychological scientists have found that one of the most effective coping strategies is social support, that is, turning to the comfort and contact of other people. Social support makes us less anxious and depressed, and it even makes us healthier. We should now turn to our friends, our partners, our colleagues, companions, and confidants. They will give us room to share our feelings, to belong, and to discover that we are not alone.

4. Traumatic and painful experiences can shake our most basic assumptions about the world. The Bush presidency may have made you ask the Big Questions: Why us? How can we prevent this type of situation from recurring? And, if you're religious, How

could God let it happen? Countless studies show that this process can be difficult and painful but ultimately quite valuable.

5. In my research, I have found that one of the most powerful strategies for becoming a happier person is the regular expression of gratitude. For example, experimental happiness "interventions" have revealed that people who practice gratitude once a week, either by counting their blessings or by writing letters of gratitude to the people in their lives who have been kind to them—but whom they have never properly thanked—become happier over time and experience increases in their sense of connection with others.

   This work suggests that we should try to focus not on what we *don't* have but on what we *do* have. To help us recover from the W years, we should focus our attention on the people, things, ideas, and events that have made our personal lives and our larger world a better place.

6. I don't mean to suggest that we should all try to look back on the Bush years through rose-colored spectacles. We should be realistic but also recognize our strengths, and then rise to the occasion and go forward with an energetic and optimistic spirit.

Congratulations! You have made it through all twelve steps. You are now stronger than before, ready to venture into the world, no longer suffering from your George W. Bush–induced insanity, and eager to help others recover. Remission accomplished!

ACKNOWLEDGMENTS

Writing an instant book means making a lot of instant friends and relying on old ones. After three weeks, I've forgotten which are which. But I'm pretty sure that if it weren't for the following people, this book wouldn't have been anything close to instant: Tracy Behar, David Blum, Susan Crile, Mark Davis, Rip Esselstyn, Dan Frank, Jim Howe, Rick Kot, Johannis Loldrup, Arthur Lubow, Barbara Marcus, Glenn Sinclair, Jim Stewart, Daniel Wheeler, Don Wiesberg, and Rafe Yglesias. Then there are the Columbia Journalism School grads, thanks to the heroic efforts of Zeb Esselstyn: Conn Corrigan, Elizabeth Dwoskin, Indu Nepal, Craig Rothstein, Alexa Schirtzinger, Alex Sundby, Kim Thorpe, Laurence Witherington, and especially Josh Zembik.

My agent, Richard Pine, is a saint.

Many contributors took time out of their lives to think about the last eight years, and were still willing to write something: Gail Evans, James Gleick, Dan Greenburg, Greg Greene, Frederick Hammond, John Hartmann, Tony Hendra, Jonathan Z. Larsen, Mark Liponis, Sonja Lyubomirsky, Nathan Richardson, Andy Tobias, Mel White, and Matt Yglesias. I owe them all.

Nothing would have happened without Carl Pritzkat

and Tony Travostino, who did more than help. They wrote. Also, as always, Miranda Spencer.

At Random House I'd like to thank my excellent editor Bruce Tracy and his assistant Ryan Doherty, and Kate Blum, Benjamin Dreyer, Lisa Feuer, Laura Goldin, Mark Maguire, Elizabeth McGuire, Beth Pearson, Beck Stvan, and Lisa Turner.

Finally, if you'd like to read a real recovery or 12-step book rather than a parody, two excellent choices are *The Recovery Book* by Al J. Mooney and *Understanding the Twelve Steps* by Terence T. Gorski.

ABOUT THE AUTHOR

GENE STONE is the author of the *New York Times* best-seller *The Bush Survival Bible* and *Duck!: The Dick Cheney Survival Bible*. A former book, magazine, and newspaper editor, as well as the author or ghostwriter of more than thirty books, he divides his time between Manhattan, upstate New York, and worrying about the planet.